AUTHOR BIOGRAPHY

Sarah lives and works on a former strawberry farm in Essex. Here, she and her husband Dale Gibson run their sustainable beekeeping practice, Bermondsey Street Bees, garden in all weathers and take their dogs on wild coastal walks.

A key element of their beekeeping has always been to promote best practice beekeeping, maintaining environmental balance between managed and wild bee populations. This extends into collaborating on many educational and scientific projects and the pollinator gardens they've created in private and public spaces.

A professional writer and speaker, Sarah appears widely in print, online and at international events. Her first book *Planting for Honeybees* (Quadrille, 2018) remains a bestseller in both the UK and USA.

Through her advocacy for bee welfare and sustainable honey production, Sarah is also well-known in the food world as a honey expert and active proponent of the global Slow Food movement.

bermondseystreetbees.co.uk
@plantingforthebees

CONTENTS

INTRODUCTION

An only, but never lonely, child, I spent endless hours observing nature – stretched out on my grandmother's terrace in Spain during feverishly-hot afternoons watching ant nests (never a dull moment in the ant world!), seeking toads lurking golden-eyed by the ponds on London's Hampstead Heath, or gathering miniature sea snails from the foreshore in Scotland.

An attempt to keep snails in a salvaged Nescafé tin in my bedroom ended when grown-ups tracked down the source of an appalling smell taking over the house. Many of my experiments in 'taming' wildlife ended similarly – in being told to put it back – but my curiosity was always encouraged. Small or large, the truly wild is never predictable and therein lay the attraction. (History repeats itself: from grasshoppers to snakes and crabs, my two sons were also both passionate bringers-home of small creatures.)

As with many children without siblings, I lived an intense life of my own in parallel with the life of my large extended family, but would often attach myself to relatives when they were doing something interesting. Usually that was outdoors, trailing my grandfather, thirsty for his knowledge about everything we saw or heard.

My grandfather had kept bees for many years but by the time I knew him, the skeps sat empty in a shed (woven of straw, they made terrific helmets when my cousins and I staged mock battles). But his love and knowledge of bees – all bees – was immense and, like his gardening, extremely interactive.

He cosseted and cajoled plants into flowering, sometimes even giving them strict lectures (he was a former naval officer and gardening was no whimsical pastime). Together, though, we quietly observed the less obvious life of the garden – the field mice in the shed, the mallards nesting in the oak tree and the visiting bees. When I was very small, he showed me that worn-out bees could often be rescued and revived (see page 122), which seemed a magical process. I was

fascinated by bumblebees' amazing 'hooky' feet, which allowed them to peacefully anchor on to a human hand just as well as any flower. All bee species share the same feet, but not the tendency to interact so placidly.

Shadowing him through spring and summer days, on walks or working in the garden, I also learned to differentiate some wild bee species, particularly, as he taught me, by watching specific plants they favoured and places they liked to nest. Identification was not always easy, though, with around 250 different types of bee in the UK alone (and a staggering 25,000 species worldwide).

Sadly, what's written about bees in the mainstream media today is mostly far too generalized and usually partly or wholly wrong. Mostly, too, it is focused on honeybees, ignoring the countless wild bee species that also contribute so much. Even at a government level, pollinator policy-making has for decades been dominated by honeybee priorities – as if everything said of them was also true for multiple different species. Or even worse, as if they were the only bees that mattered.

All bees are not the same and generalities are unhelpful. We need an informed, holistic and constructive approach to understanding our wild bees, the issues they face in the modern world, and what we can do to help them survive.

It was similarly muddy generalities that led me to research and write my first book, *Planting for Honeybees*, setting out to sort fact from fiction as I established new pollinator gardens in our Suffolk bee yard and on our London roof terrace. As professional beekeepers, my husband Dale and I have always been clear about our responsibility to 'green offset' the impact of our beehives on local wild bee populations that share the same floral resources. For nearly two decades we have planted wherever we live and work, and mentored the creation of pollinator gardens in many different countries. Our experience informs this new book.

The decline in global insect numbers is acknowledged as a key indicator of environmental crisis, but I'm reduced to headshaking disbelief at how the popular messaging persistently ignores the most beneficial of

insects; the wild bees. Plenty is said about stresses on honeybees, but not nearly enough people know anything about their even more vulnerable cousins, which is why I now want to shine a light specifically on them.

I'm writing this book at a turning point in my life, as we have finally made a permanent move from London eastwards out to coastal Essex. Rather than having to beg, steal and borrow patches to plant, I suddenly have a huge garden, which makes me feel quite panicky! I want to do everything, and I want to do it now. The reality is that it will take years to build up the ecosystem that until now has been mainly in my imaginings. But there's already a rich variety of bee and other pollinator species here and I'm working hard to learn how to differentiate and support them through specific planting and natural habitat creation.

So your journey through this book is my journey too. Whether you'd like to enjoy some more knowledgeable bee spotting or whether you have space to plant and create habitat, the very fact of knowing more about the incredible diversity of bees and their amazing life stories makes an important contribution to the wider understanding that we so badly need.

A WORD ABOUT NUMBERS

Nature doesn't lend itself to head counts. But wanting to give context, numbers are useful, so I've mostly used consensus rather than always prefacing with 'approximately'.

Hence, there are usually said to be 25,000 species of bee on earth. It's changeable though, with reclassifications, extinctions, and new discoveries. And how many honeybee species are there globally? I'm saying seven. That's the figure most widely used, as is the 250 species of bumblebee. And that bumblebee queen? Does she always measure 16 mm (½ in)? No, she could be as big as 22 mm (¾ in). Mutability within the natural world is part of the joy of discovery.

CHAPTER 1

—

ALL BEES
Are Not the Same

ALL BEES ARE NOT THE SAME

*The way the media have it, there is really only one bee
– the honeybee. The bee that makes our breakfast honey.*

Radiant in the glory of their special talent, honeybees have become the sentimental proxy for all bees, dominating the headlines and mopping up all the bee love going. Complicating things further, few people know what a honeybee is, or looks like. Shown pictures of honeybees and bumblebees and asked which one makes the honey, most (wrongly) select the furry bumblebee, because it looks so 'cute', especially compared to its slightly waspy-looking cousin, the famous honeybee.

Again, the media has a lot to answer for in persistently sowing seeds of ignorance. Countless honeybee-themed books, films, jewellery, stationery, beauty products and food packaging (sometimes even honey jars) feature images of bumblebees, because they are so adorably rounded and furry; everyone's 'ideal' bee. This makes about as much sense as illustrating stories about rhinos with pictures of elephants – yes, both are big and grey, but they're completely different animals.

Likewise, all bees are not the same. In fact, there are as many as 25,000 different bee species on earth. But out of that enormous number, only seven species are honeybees, representing 0.03 per cent of the totality of global bee species. The UK numbers around 250 different bees and the US has 4,000 plus. Both though, have just one species of honey bee – of which just one is a honeybee.

Shocked? Here's another big surprise.

No matter what the media and marketeers say, honeybees, although sometimes grievously exploited by humans, are not facing extinction. This is because, just like chickens or sheep, they are a farmed species, making their numbers largely human managed. Where hives are lost (through factors such as poor management, hunger, disease and/ or other environmental pressures) they can be replaced through breeding programmes.

Far from becoming extinct, global numbers of managed honeybees have been rising steadily over the decades, despite even the US's 'colony collapse' crisis, first reported in 2006. (See United Nations' chart on page 14).

Numbers continue to increase, with an informally estimated 94 million hives in 2021. Many hives provide commercial pollination services or valuable income to subsistence farmers in developing regions. But increasing numbers of environmentalists identify this density of (often imported) honeybees as a growing challenge to native wild bee and other pollinator species, which are forced to share shrinking resources in ever more fragile environments. Several bumblebee species are also commercially farmed and shipped globally to boost crop pollination (see pages 49–53). These, of course, have escaped into the wild, in some places devastating native bee populations.

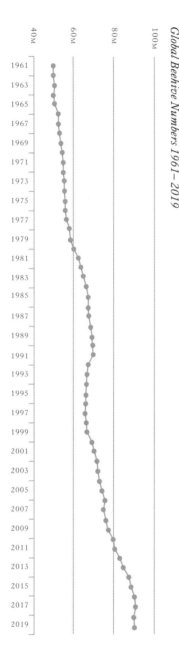

Global Beehive Numbers 1961–2019

100M	80M	60M	40M

1961
1963
1965
1967
1969
1971
1973
1975
1977
1979
1981
1983
1985
1987
1989
1991
1993
1995
1997
1999
2001
2003
2005
2007
2009
2011
2013
2015
2017
2019

SOURCE: UNITED NATIONS
(FAOSTAT)

But because the majority of wild bees don't offer humans the obvious allure of commercial manageability, their life cycles often pass unseen, with little public understanding of the specific habitat and forage upon which they depend. They are just 'there', as part of nature's great plan. Except that, increasingly, they are no longer there.

Wild bee species are essential pollinators, yet many are at significant risk from rapid changes in land use and the ever-onward marches of urbanization and big farming practices. So you can see why we urgently need to broaden the bee debate. When news headlines and marketing boffins shout out that tired mantra 'Save the bees', we should all be asking 'Which bees, and where?'.

I'm hoping this book will give you a greater understanding of bees, topple misleading myths, and provide practical ideas to support our amazingly diverse and fascinating bee populations. We can't individually change the world, but if enough of us take enough small positive actions, either through knowing or doing, they add up to something meaningful and significant.

There are many people out there fighting hard to save our wild bees and I hope you will join them. Change your focus from macro to micro, and the world around you will also change.

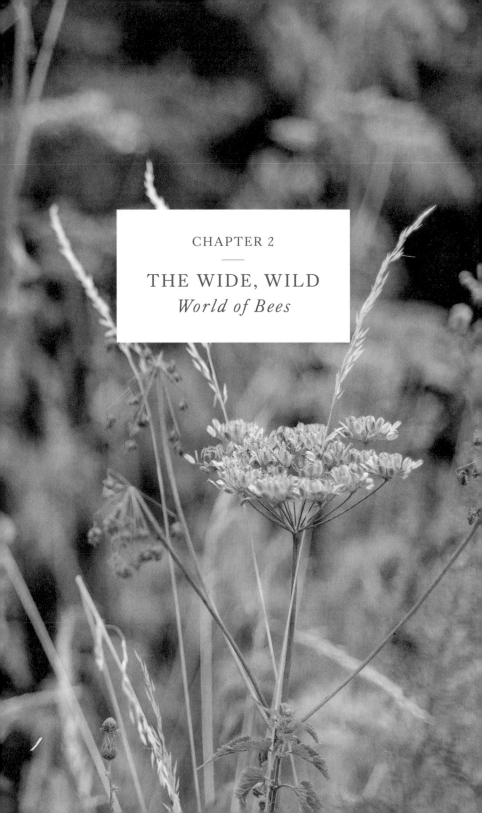

CHAPTER 2

—

THE WIDE, WILD
World of Bees

THE WIDE, WILD WORLD OF BEES

There are around 25,000 bee species on this planet. That's more than all mammal, bird and amphibian species added together.

Bees are truly ancient, having evolved from common wasp ancestors between 80 and 90 million years ago. In that time they've weathered everything the planet has thrown at them – perhaps, that is, until now, as the massed pressures of modern farming, urbanization, widespread chemical use and climate change prove too much for many insects.

Bees of all species share a basic physical form. The majority gather ultra-fine pollen grains and nectar (a sweet substance exuded by plants), both of which are food resources. While visiting flowers to collect these, they incidentally pollinate the plants on which so much of nature depends. Their work as pollinators makes them vital to this planet. And that's about the sum total of generalizations we should ever make about bees, because every bee species has its own unique physical appearance and life cycle, its own specific habitat needs, and its own nutritional requirements.

Science groups bees into families, but the simplest division to make is between the socials and the solitaries.

THE SOCIAL BEES

Social bees live in colonies comprising a queen bee, female workers and males. Very few bee species are social, principally the seven honeybee species, the 250 species of bumblebee and around 500 species of stingless bee.

Stingless bees, native to tropical and sub-tropical regions, are the only other bee species kept by humans specifically to produce honey (albeit a very different kind of honey, produced in minute quantities). Honeybees and stingless bees both live in large, long-lived colonies, supported through tough times (winter, monsoon, drought and so on) by their honey stores. Their queens may live for several years.

A bumblebee queen, however, generally only lives for an annual cycle, during which she builds up a relatively small colony that is completely dispersed within just a few months. In temperate climates, her late-season daughters (new queens) mate in autumn and then hibernate alone before starting their own individual colonies the following spring. However, climate change is starting to affect patterns of bumblebee hibernation in temperate climates.

THE SOLITARY BEES

Around 90 per cent of the world's bees are solitary species, including mason bees, mining bees and many others. Their life cycles are short and, depending on their species, they may burrow underground or make their nests in hollow plant stems or holes in wood or brick. As you'll discover on pages 151–158, some are even more creative in their choice of home.

Solitary bees generally live alone, with no queen bee and no workers. Each female builds her own very particular type of nest, gathers the specific nutrition that her brood needs and lays her eggs into well-stocked larders before sealing and leaving the nest. She dies, leaving her offspring to emerge several months later and start the solitary cycle again. The young male bees tend to leave the nest first so that they are matured and ready to mate when the young females emerge slightly later. Each female then seeks out a good place near to forage sources to build her own nest.

While it can sometimes seem as if you have a 'colony' of solitary bees, this is only because some species happily site their individual nests close together if there's an attractive area of habitat. (But just to confuse things further, scientists have identified a few solitaries that exhibit primitive social behaviours.)

CUCKOO BEES

Many bee species are susceptible to having their colonies infiltrated by parasitic 'cuckoo' bees, which lay their eggs in their chosen host's nest. It's a clever strategy, taking advantage of a willing workforce in the case of bumblebees and abundantly stocked larders in the case of solitary bees.

Bumblebee species often have their own specific 'lookalike' cuckoo bees. A convincing resemblance and clever timing are both essential to their sneaky tactics. Seeking to either live alongside or kill and replace the legitimate bumblebee queen, a cuckoo female needs to enter the host nest without being spotted and despatched by the workforce. Once accepted, she can install herself as a new and legitimate queen, lay her eggs and allow the worker bumblebees to feed and raise her cuckoo brood for her.

Nature's pragmatism may seem harsh, but it is all about maintaining balance. Each of these insects has its own allotted role within the bigger picture.

< *Different bee species can happily co-exist, occupying different habitats within a single environment*

'GENERALIZED' BEE ANATOMY

Bee body shapes, sizes and colours differ widely,
but they share a basic anatomy

Bees have two pairs of wings:

Hind wing   *Fore wing*

*Narrow
'wasp waist'*

Thorax   *3x Ocelli
(simple eyes for
light detection)*

*Spiracle
(breathing hole)*

*Large compound
eyes set on either
side of head*

Abdomen

*Antennae with
receptors for
touch, taste, smell,
temperature,
humidity and
wind speed*

*Stinger
(if bee has one)*

*Mandibles
(jaws)*

Hind leg

Middle leg

*Proboscis
(retractable
'drinking
straw' tongue)*

*Tarsal Claw – each
leg terminates in
a tarsal claw
which can move
through many
angles, Ideal for
clinging to flowers
and rough*

*Location of pollen basket
(corbicle) on bees which
have them. Many other
species have 'scopae';
areas of bristly hairs on
their body which trap
grains of pollen*

Foreleg

WHAT *do* BEES CONTRIBUTE TO LIFE ON EARTH?

Pollination activity by the world's 25,000 different bee species directly provides millions of living creatures with food, including fruits, nuts and vegetables. Pollination also creates plant habitats that support incalculable numbers of organisms, from the most primitive to the most complex. Here are some of the lesser -known contributions that bees make:

MEAT AND DAIRY PRODUCTS

Feed given to cows, sheep and pigs, either in dried pellet form or as silage, includes bee-pollinated plants, such as clover, alfalfa, soybeans and peas. Poultry feed often includes a component of these crops, and chickens are sometimes fed calendula petals to colour the yolks of their eggs a rich yellow.

Grazing chickens and ruminants often feed on bee-pollinated plants too. There has also been a resurgence in farmers using traditional crop rotations that include 'herbal leys' – complex mixtures of different grasses with bee-pollinated herbs and legumes. These naturally enrich the soil, boost the health of grazing animals, provide rich forage for pollinators, and greatly reduce agrichemical use.

Without bees, our meat, eggs and dairy products would be greatly diminished in nutritional and flavour quality, and so scarce as to be unaffordable or unavailable to most people.

FISH

The pelletized foods that feed farmed fish contain bee-pollinated products, including soybeans and rapeseed (canola) oil.

MEDICINES

Traditional systems of medicine have always relied on bee-pollinated plants, from potent herbs to the bark and leaves of trees; from draughts, salves and tinctures to essential oils. But modern medicine places equal reliance on bee-pollinated plants. They are needed to create important

White-tailed bumblebees nested happily under my garden shed,
going in and out through a crack between the stone step and the wall

pain remedies such as morphine (from opium poppies), aspirin (from willow bark) and capsaicin (from chilli peppers). Vinca (periwinkle) is used in lifesaving anti-cancer drugs, artemisia extracts are used to treat drug-resistant malaria, and the common snowdrop provides an alkaloid used in the treatment of Alzheimer's. The list goes on and on, taking folk medicine into modern pharmacology.

TIMBER

Much of the quality timber used for furniture and construction comes from hardwood trees, which are visited and pollinated by bees.

FABRICS

Some important natural fibres come from bee-pollinated plants; from cotton and linen to hemp and sisal.

HORTICULTURAL SEED PRODUCTION

The seeds we buy for our gardens come largely from plants pollinated by bees.

THE KITCHEN STORE CUPBOARD

Alongside the multitude of fruits and vegetables with which the bees provide us, our kitchen cupboards are full of bee-pollinated products.

Spices: Bees play a role in producing thousands of seasonings and flavourings, including saffron, cardamom, allspice, vanilla, nutmeg, star anise, tamarind and mustard.

Herbs: The majority of the obvious kitchen (and medicinal) herbs are bee-pollinated. These include basil, thyme, rosemary, oregano, sage, mint, chives, bay, coriander (cilantro) as well as the including thousands of lesser-known wild herbs.

Oils: Rapeseed (canola), flaxseed (linseed) and sunflower oil all come from bee-pollinated crops.

Little luxuries: Coffee, tea and, to a lesser extent, chocolate all involve bees in their production.

FROM EGG *to* ADULT

However different their subsequent life cycles may be, all bees share basic stages as they grow from egg to adult. Solitary bees can take months to complete their metamorphosis from egg to adult while social bees make the transition far more quickly, in just a few weeks.

EGG

Eggs that hatch to produce young female bees are laid by adult females who have mated and hold sperm reserves in their bodies. They use this sperm to fertilize the eggs which grow into daughters.

Eggs intended to produce *male bees* are purposely left unfertilized. This means that in social bee colonies, male eggs can sometimes be laid by unmated workers.

In social colonies, eggs are laid into cells made with wax produced by the bees' bodies and the worker bees painstakingly tend the brood. By contrast, solitary bee females lay into food-stocked cells they've constructed from leaves, mud or other materials. The nest is then sealed, leaving the next generation to fend for itself.

LARVA TO PREPUPA

The eggs hatch into larvae (the time this takes varies by species). Lacking legs and eyes, these are tiny curled-up grubs that look completely different from adult bees.

Larvae feed voraciously and typically shed their skin repeatedly as they grow. In social colonies, workers provide them with quantities of pollen moistened with nectar, which is brought in regularly by foraging bees. In solitary bee species, the larvae feed themselves from the food laid down by the female before she sealed each cell. Eventually larvae stop feeding before they enter the pupal stage, their next step towards adulthood.

PUPA TO ADULT

Most bee larvae pupate inside silky cocoons that they spin themselves (though there are exceptions and some species have eliminated this stage altogether). Inside a cocoon, the juvenile matures into its fully adult form before finally eating its way out of its cell. Exposure to air hardens off its soft body and it becomes a functional adult bee.

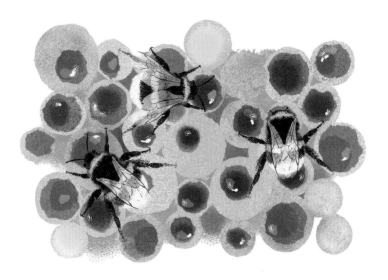

Bumblebees build wax cells and 'honey pots' within their nests

How bees and humans see the same dandelion

WHAT DO BEES SEE, SMELL AND HEAR?

SIGHT

Bees experience the world around them in a different way to humans, starting with what they see with their two sets of eyes. The large compound eyes situated on either side of their head are made up of numerous lenses that individually send messages in mosaic form to the brain, which constructs them into whole images. They detect movement faster than the human eye.

The colour perception of their compound eyes is different from ours, as bees see into the ultra-violet spectrum. Many flowers use colours invisible to the human eye to give specific information to bees about their form or their forage potential. Most bees have a distinct preference for blue or purple flowers, with yellow and white also highly visible to them. Red flowers appear black to a bee.

On the top of their head are three far more primitive eyes called ocelli or eye spots, each one a single lens. Arranged in a triangle, these allow bees to orientate themselves using the sun, even on cloudy days. Many other types of insects also have ocelli, including cockroaches and flies.

Bees depend heavily on sight when outside the nest, and young bees in social colonies can be seen making orientation flights, memorising their surroundings before becoming foragers. As well as orienting themselves in relation to the sun, all bee species see and memorize physical landmarks to lead them safely out and back on foraging or mating flights.

Studies show that honeybees can use these same skills to identify human faces, recognizing them (as we do) from multiple different viewpoints and remembering them for up to two days. See pages 31–32 or more information on bee intelligence.

Bees have yet another way of navigating, using electroreceptors in their bodies to receive data about where they are. They can also use electromagnetic signals from plants and hydrocarbon 'footprints' left by other bees to pick up information about forage availability.

SMELL AND TASTE

A keen sense of smell is vital to bees. Olfactory receptors on their antennae help locate attractive forage sources, sometimes miles away. Social bees' relationships are dominated by smell. Bumblebee and honeybee queens control their nests via the release of pheromones (natural chemicals). The queen's smell is spread throughout the nest by the workers, creating a badge of belonging and dictating the actions and temperament of the colony. So powerful is it that it even controls the physical development of the female workers, preventing their ovaries from developing.

As a bumblebee queen's pheromones fade at the end of her life cycle, her control diminishes. Her daughter workers may then seize control of the nest and, with their ovaries now active, lay their own (unfertilized) eggs.

Honeybees respond to a failing queen's pheromones by replacing her with a new young queen (see pages 116–119). Once mated, the new queen will sting her predecessor to death, unless the previous queen has already left the nest at the heart of a swarm. Pheromones also play a key role in mating behaviours, attracting females to specific places where congregations of male bees await.

Bees also have a good sense of taste. Sensors situated in their antennae, mouth parts and front feet are well attuned to assessing sweetness and, in tests conducted with honeybees, saltiness too.

HEARING

Bees do not have ears, but they do hear by picking up vibrations through specialist organs on their legs and antennae. Their whole body is also extremely sensitive to vibrations, whether they are transmitted through the air or via a surface.

Not having ears limits the sound frequencies bees can detect, but they can 'hear' loud sounds and human voices. However, for bees, hearing is a way of ensuring survival, not about social interaction, so what they are good at detecting primarily concerns their forage, mating and other essential behaviours.

The buzzing of bees is created by the movement of their wings via their thoracic flight muscles and allows them to transmit information or requests to one another. Honeybees (but not bumblebees) can accompany this with 'dancing' in their nest, using the comb to amplify specific vibrations. Young queen honeybees also create another noise that is clearly audible to humans and is often described as 'piping' or 'tooting'.

Bees have survived for more than 80 million years because they are incredibly adaptable. At the root of their adaptability is the ability to learn. Naturalists, philosophers, sociologists, behavioural scientists and many other experts share a fascination with the complexity of bees' lives, especially the colony-building social bees. The success of the colony – which is, effectively, a single organism – depends on every individual in that organism fulfilling its given role at a given time.

As well as the obvious motor skills, this involves sophisticated physical perception of the world around them. Social bees have the ability to communicate their findings to each other in various ways (see opposite), and to act in response to that information. All bees also have profound connections with the plants on which they feed, involving, at the very least, subtle visual and scent cues that dictate the bees' subsequent behaviour.

There's a combination of inherited knowledge and on-the-spot learning at play here, and in recent years scientists have been testing bee brain power in some novel ways. Several studies have used rewards to induce bees to visit specially coloured or even artificial 'flowers'. The bees quickly learned to associate positive outcomes with particular forms and/ or colours, giving us a glimpse of their agility in adapting to changing environments and flora.

Bees also learn from each other, as shown by research in which scientists trained bumblebees to differentiate and manipulate small yellow balls and find sugar water rewards. Their sister bumblebees watching the experiment learned what to do by sight alone, going on to improve the techniques they used to manipulate both the target yellow ball and a replacement ball of a different colour. As one of the researchers at Queen Mary University of London commented, 'It puts the final nail in the coffin of the idea that small brains constrain insects.' You can watch a wonderful video of the Queen Mary University researchers' bumblebee training on YouTube.[1]

Honeybee colonies are longer lived and their societies even more complex than the lives of bumblebees. As a species, they are said to be the second-most widely studied living creature – the first being humans. We remain fascinated by their abilities, both instinctive and learned. Recently, Sheffield University researchers discovered that honeybees could solve maths challenges using visual cues rather than the cognitive number processing used by human brains. This is said to be significant both for future developments in artificial intelligence (AI) and for a new understanding of many other creatures' numerical abilities. Honeybees' acute sense of smell has also led to scientists training them to sniff out landmines.

On the home front, we've seen the bees in our own hives showing a behaviour clearly learned hundreds of thousands of years ago and never forgotten. To a honeybee, any brown furry animal near its nest is a bear intent on stealing its honey. So while the bees in our home apiary peacefully tolerate our sleek, white cat waggling his paw into their hive entrances, our chocolate brown Burmese regularly comes tearing into the house after being seen off by cross bees. He has learned to keep his distance, as has our shaggy brown retriever, while our little black pug can potter unbothered through the apiary.

Our 'Bee Dogs': Midge, the bear, and Moss the pug

WHAT'S THE DIFFERENCE
BETWEEN NECTAR AND HONEY?

Bees collect nectar from plants. They suck this sugary-sweet, watery substance from flowers using their proboscis (a drinking straw-like mouthpart) and keep it in a special honey stomach for the journey back to their nest. Nectar-producing plants usually have internal nectar-producing glands (nectaries) housed within the flower, but some, including bracken, elderberry and passion flower plants, have external nectaries on their stems or leaves.

In bumblebee nests, the nectar is stored in tiny wax pots. Adult bees draw from it and worker bees mix a little in with the pollen that they feed to the brood. Solitary bees also feed on nectar and blend it with pollen, leaving the mixture close to their eggs as food for their emerging larvae. Both bumblebees and solitary bees have short-lived nests, so do not need to lay down large stores. Nor do they need to worry about the moisture level in the nectar (which can be as much as 80 per cent water) leading it to ferment. It will be used up long before that happens.

Honeybees, though, have large colonies that live from year to year. Like bumblebees and solitary bees, they gather nectar for adults and brood. Vitally, they also store it in large quantities in the comb they build, laying down larders to draw upon in bad weather or through winter when the colony huddles around its precious queen. To build up this volume of stores, honeybees need to gather a great deal more nectar than other bees, which makes them hyper-attuned to nectar-yielding flowers.

To prevent the nectar fermenting, honeybees reduce its water content dramatically before storing it in the comb, concentrating the dilute sugars into the viscous, naturally-sterile supersaturate that we call honey. Much of the dehydration is accomplished by fanning their wings over the nectar-packed cells, creating the 'hum' we hear from a busy hive.

Only when they have reduced the water content to around 18 per cent will they put the final wax capping on their honey storage cells. (The tropical/sub-tropical stingless bee species also gather nectar and make a very liquid version of honey, stored within the colony in tiny wax pots.)

As the stored honey is so concentrated, honeybees may need to transport small amounts of water into their nest to dilute or dissolve it before feeding. Bumblebees and solitary species are less dependent on external water supplies, as the nectar they consume already has a high water content.

Honey is the extraordinary nourishment that allows honeybee (and stingless bee) colonies to survive tough times. Responsible beekeepers never remove their bees' vital stores, only ever taking production that is clearly surplus to the hive's needs. Wild bee colonies may, of course, have to defend their stores against an even longer list of potential honey-robbers than managed hives.

NOT A BEE AT ALL

As if life wasn't complicated enough for the would-be bee spotter, there is a vast array of other insects that naturally resemble or have set out to mimic bees.

Black-and-yellow body colouring advertises toxicity or aggression throughout the insect world, so many insects (including peaceful and harmless ones) have evolved to resemble bees or wasps to either protect themselves from predators (a type of imitation known as 'Batesian mimicry') or pull off other confidence tricks.

Here are the three main types of insects commonly mistaken for bee:

WASPS AND HORNETS

People often confuse wasps and honeybees because they share the black-and-yellow stripes of their common ancestry. But they have evolved very differently and when you see them side by side they are obviously not the same creature. Bees have furrier bodies and their markings are muted compared to the vivid yellow stripes of a wasp. Unlike wasps, bees are vegetarian and have no interest in human food (unless you have an open honey pot on the table). It is wasps, not bees, that can make outdoor eating a misery in summer.

Not surprisingly, we humans react badly to these persistent and aggressive wasps joining our picnics and barbecues. We fear their stings and question what useful function they can possibly serve. In fact, wasps are extraordinarily important insects whose role in nature is increasingly better understood and valued by scientists.

There are over 100,000 different wasp species (of which few are bothersome to us). Like bees, some are social and live in large colonies, but the majority are solitary. They are useful pollinators, but most importantly, their carnivorous eating habits help keep numbers of potentially overwhelming pests, such as caterpillars, in check. Without wasp predation, many valuable crops would be lost to munching pests. The Natural History Museum notes that there are over 7,000 different

Honeybee   *Wasp*

wasp species in the UK alone, estimating that between them they eat over 14 million kg (15½ tons) of insect prey per annum.

Hornets are the largest of the social wasps, with approximately 20 species worldwide. They are often extremely aggressive, and their stings are more toxic than those of other wasps or bees. They also are vital wild pest control work, but have become problematic invaders in some regions.

The majority of hornets originate from Asia, but the native European hornet has found ways to make itself at home in North America too. Likewise Asian hornets, which are far more aggressive, have hitched a lift to Europe and the UK and their range, in both rural and urban areas, is spreading despite government-mandated controls.

They are significant predators of honeybees and their presence causes major issues for beekeepers. Entire hives can be wiped out by Asian hornets first snatching bees on the wing and then overwhelming the weakened colony in a matter of hours. North America has similar problems with another incomer, the giant Japanese hornet. Headlined 'the murder hornet', it is a huge insect with a body around 4.5 cm (1¾ in) long, a wingspan of 7.5 cm (3 in) and particularly potent venom. A definite avoid if possible.

HOVER FLIES

Bee imitator spotting can be just as much fun as spotting the bees themselves. At first glance, many flies make pretty good bee mimics, but they are betrayed by two physical characteristics – their extremely large fly eyes, which virtually meet on the top of their head, and not having that ultra-slender 'wasp waist' shared by all bees and wasps. With closer inspection, you can also see that hover flies have one set of wings, where as bees have two.

Most bee-mimicking flies are hover flies (which do literally hover, like mini helicopters). They don't bite or sting and are a benign and useful presence in the garden. Like bees, they feed on pollen and nectar and are recognized as a key group of pollinating insects. But unlike bees, their larvae feed on insects such as aphids, thrips, scale bugs and caterpillars, keeping pest populations in check. The 6,000+ species of hoverfly (250+ in the UK and almost 900 in the US) are one of the best examples of Batesian mimicry. Among the most convincing hover flies are those that specifically mimic bumblebees, and the 'drone-flies' which do a great job of pretending to be male honeybees.

BEE FLIES

Another exponent of Batesian mimicry, bee flies have distinctive pear-shaped bodies (often with a bumblebee-like fuzz) and a long spiny-looking fixed proboscis. They also have long, spindly legs; very different from any bee.

There are around 5,000 known bee fly species in the world (nine in the UK and around 800 in the US). They, too, gather pollen and nectar, making them excellent pollinators as they nip from flower to flower. Their larvae feed on the eggs and larvae of other insects and to ensure good food sources, some species of bee fly locate their eggs in the burrows of beetles, wasps, solitary bees or other hosts. Some types of bee fly are associated with a specific host species, others are less discriminating.

Many solitary bees are targeted by insect tricksters deploying mimicry and stealth. The dark-edged bee fly, for instance, sneaks

Hover fly   *Bee fly*

up on mining bees' nest holes, cunningly weighting its eggs with soil before flicking them into the nest. Once the cuckoo species' eggs hatch, they'll make their way into the nest chambers to finish their development by feasting on the bodily fluids of the developing larvae of the mining bee hosts.

BEE OR FLY?

Some visual pointers

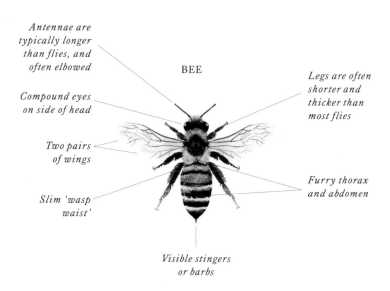

Antennae are typically longer than flies, and often elbowed

BEE

Legs are often shorter and thicker than most flies

Compound eyes on side of head

Two pairs of wings

Furry thorax and abdomen

Slim 'wasp waist'

Visible stingers or barbs

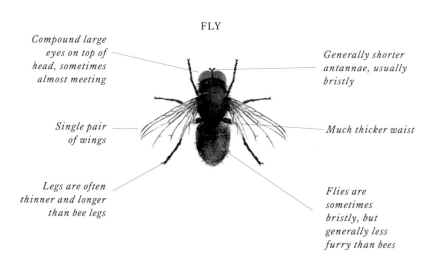

FLY

Compound large eyes on top of head, sometimes almost meeting

Generally shorter antannae, usually bristly

Single pair of wings

Much thicker waist

Legs are often thinner and longer than bee legs

Flies are sometimes bristly, but generally less furry than bees

CHAPTER 3

—

POLLINATION,
POLLINATORS &
PROBLEMS

POLLINATION, POLLINATORS
& PROBLEMS

What is pollination and why is it so vital? Experts chat blithely about 'pollinators' as if everyone has complete understanding of this whole topic, but speaking for myself, I haven't revisited the technicalities of the process since my schooldays, and I'll bet many people have never had any opportunity to dig into the subject. So here is a quick overview.

Pollination is, very simply, how flowering plants reproduce. The ability of plants to reproduce successfully is one of the cornerstones of nature. Without plant reproduction, life on earth would be finished. Plants shape and maintain this planet, feed its occupants, take in carbon dioxide and release the oxygen we breathe.

Pollinators are animals that unwittingly transfer pollen between plants, allowing pollination to occur. Insects – from bees, beetles and moths to wasps and flies – are the best known of these, but birds, bats and many small mammals are also pollinators. Globally, over 90 per cent of wild plants and 75 per cent of common crops depend on insect and other animal pollination.

THE POLLINATION PROCESS

Typically, pollen grains produced by the male part of a flower (the stamen, with its anthers set on slim filaments) are transferred by pollinators or other means to the female pistil (composed of stigma, style and ovary). The pollen, which sticks to the stigma, contains male gametes (sperm).

The pollen grows a tube down the length of the female style to the ovary at its base, which contains female gametes (ovules). Via this tube, the male gametes fertilize the ovules, which become seeds, held within a fruit or other casing formed by the ovary. The seeds then grow to create the next generation of the plant.

Plants that have evolved flowers and produce enclosed seeds in this way are called *angiosperms*. This is as opposed to the non-flowering *gymnosperms*, which are less highly evolved, generally wind-pollinated plants, such as conifers. Gymnosperm seeds, such as pine cones, are called 'naked', because they lack a surrounding casing, such as a nut or berry.

Angiosperms make up about 80 per cent of all known living plant species on earth and the majority of them depend on animal pollination.

Female parts   **Male parts**

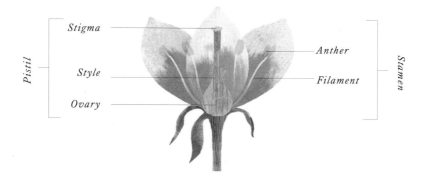

Stigma — *Anther*

Pistil — *Style* — *Filament* — *Stamen*

Ovary

Cross section of stylised plant with both male and female parts

DIFFERENT ASPECTS OF POLLINATION

Some plants, such as holly trees and willows, have separate male and female plants. These need to be reasonably close to each other if fertilization is to take place. Pollen is transferred from one to another in a process called cross-pollination.

Most plants, though, are bisexual, with each flower having both male and female parts, enabling self-pollination. Other species, such as courgettes (zucchini), produce separate male and female flowers on the same plant.

However, plants that can self-pollinate often prefer to cross-pollinate. Indeed many plants go to a lot of trouble to avoid self-pollinating. Some have their male and female flowers blooming at different times, others put up chemical barriers to self-fertilization. All of this is designed to increase the likelihood of natural cross-pollination, which builds diversity and generally breeds healthier offspring.

Plant breeders working on 'improving' species selectively cross-pollinate to create specialist hybrids with particular characteristics. As a result of selective breeding by humans, many flowering plants commonly found in gardens have moved so far away from their natural form that they become of no use to pollinators, having lost scent, nectaries (specialist nectar-secreting plant glands) and pollen. They are also often sterile and do not produce seeds, meaning that they have to be artificially propagated through techniques such as tissue culture.

HOW DOES CROSS-POLLINATION WORK?

Pollen can be transferred from plant to plant by wind and water, or by animals. Animals account for the majority of pollination, which can occur by accident or through the plant offering rich rewards to visitors.

Over millions of years of evolution, plants have developed lures such as flowers with colour, scent and sugar-rich nectars designed to attract animal pollinators, principally insects. Some insects also learned to eat pollen, another incentive to visit flowering plants. Brushing against pollen-covered anthers as they claim their reward, insects carry the grains to other flowers, hopefully delivering a plant-to-plant species match that results in fertilization.

This process may seem random and statistically unlikely, but it works. And the odds of a pollen match are greatly increased by some insect species (including honeybees and some bumblebees) that prefer to forage on just one type of plant at a time – a habit known as floral fidelity.

Many plants have evolved specifically to attract the pollinators they most need. An exclusive relationship like this further increases the odds for the plant's next generation. Knowing these affiliations also helps us decide what to plant to support specific insect species (see pages 162–185).

WHAT MAKES BEES SUCH GREAT POLLINATORS?

Bees, in all their incredible variety, are nature's uber-pollinators, perfectly adapted to transfer pollen from plant to plant as part of a compelling co-dependence. They visit flowers to gather protein-rich pollen to feed their brood or sugar-packed nectar, which sustains both adults and brood. While they are there, grains of pollen stick to their furry bodies and get carried off to other blooms. Even in some self-pollinating flowers, they can help transfer pollen from the male stamens to the female pistils.

With thousands of species of bee of all shapes and sizes in the world, there are both generalists and specialists: those, like honeybees, which thrive on diversity of floral sources, and others whose entire life cycle centres on one particular plant. Bees that practise floral fidelity greatly increase the chance of the right pollen arriving in the right place.

Different species of bee are active at different times of year, serving a wider variety of plants than many other pollinators, and they also have a range of specialist pollen-liberating strategies. Honeybees, for instance, don't pollinate tomatoes as the pollen is too sticky for them to detach. But bumblebees and a few other bee species, including carpenter bees, can release their grains by emitting a resonant, vibrating buzz. This is known as 'buzz pollination'.

A few bee species, including honeybees and bumblebees, have corbiculae – stiff hairs surrounding a dent on their hind legs. The bees use these like shopping baskets, packing them tightly with pollen grains glued together with nectar. You can see these smooth bundles, sometimes jokingly called 'pollen pants', on the bees' legs. When the bundles are just one colour, as they always are on honeybees and some bumblebees (because they are foraging on a single type of plant), you can take a sound guess at which flower they have been working, because plants have signature-coloured pollens. Horse chestnut pollen, for instance, is a strong red, while raspberry pollen is light grey. Other colours range from almost white (chicory) to near black (poppy), with an entire palette of greens, yellows and oranges in between. This adds another level of knowledge to the fun of bee spotting. It is also extremely important to beekeepers, enabling them to work out which plants their honeybees are visiting.

Most species of wild bee don't have these baskets. A few have internal pollen stomachs, but most have scopae; dense tufts of hair on their legs or body. These anchor pollen far less tightly and it remains looking fluffy and granular. Pollination experts see this as better for pollination because the loose grains so readily drop or rub off on the next flower. However, the bees with corbiculae have furry bodies, which also pick up and drop off a lot of loose pollen.

WHAT'S GOING WRONG FOR POLLINATORS?

No matter how many campaigns are run and petitions signed, pollinator decline is not about any one single issue. It is an extremely complex, multi-layered global problem with its roots in industrialized farming, urbanization and human folly.

Study after study shows insect life in sharp decline, with some projects reporting localized falls of up to 80 per cent over just a few decades. A UK citizen science project carried out by Kent Buglife reported a nationwide reduction of nearly 60 per cent in flying insects between 2004 and 2021.

'If all mankind were to disappear, the world would regenerate back to the rich state of equilibrium that existed ten thousand years ago. If insects were to vanish, the environment would collapse into chaos.'

E.O. WILSON, US BIOLOGIST AND NATURALIST

Human life is wholly dependent on insects. They are vital for breaking down waste, controlling potentially invasive pests, providing good eating for predatory species, and pollinating the plants that feed us and give us oxygen to breathe. The loss of insects strikes right at the heart of our planet's ecosystem.

Suddenly, after around 480 million years on earth, insects can no longer keep up with the pace of change, the majority of which is human made. The pressures are multiple, but at their heart is the ever-growing number of humans and our increasing separation from nature.

In the very short time (say, 250 years) since industrialization took hold, our relationship with the natural world has changed completely, from one of respect and understanding to blind and wilful exploitation.

'We have collectively failed to engage with Nature sustainably, to the extent that our demands far exceed its capacity to supply us.'

THE DASGUPTA REVIEW

(A 2021 Independent Review On The Economics Of Biodiversity)

More people than ever before live wholly urbanized lives, divorced from the realities of nature and from the millions of organisms supporting our lives and food chains. Vital insects are either demonized as dirty creepy-crawly things or, in the case of bees and butterflies, fluffily romanticized.

Environmentalists and many other experts put the case that organic/traditionally managed land gives increased soil fertility, stronger plants and higher, more nutritious crop yields. But mass food production has grown to depend on highly mechanized, chemically-supported systems of agriculture that deplete the soil, yielding weakened crops, subject to pests and diseases. To counteract this, enormous volumes of provenly toxic and other highly suspect chemicals are routinely used in global agriculture, from fertilizers and fungicides to herbicides and assorted pesticides. Many seeds that farmers buy come pre-treated with insecticides (as do many of our garden plants and seeds, unless organically produced).

Agrichemicals affect pollinators either directly, by killing them outright, or indirectly, by polluting the soil and the water table on which the plants draw, compromising the immune systems and work abilities of visiting insects. Bees exposed to so-called 'non-fatal' levels of environmental pollutants have been shown to lose directional sense and foraging ability, compromising their viability.

The second key factor in the decline of our insect pollinators is lack of habitat and forage. Nowhere to live, nothing to eat.

For optimal financial return, big agriculture requires extremely large areas of open land, easily worked by massive machinery. Single crops can now cover miles, replacing the traditional practice of having small fields divided by nature-supporting hedges or stone walls, allowing diverse crop production, grown in rotation to build soil health and support wild organisms. In the name of progress, many countries have seen huge changes in land use, including significant deforestation, soil erosion and the destruction of specialist habitats and feeding grounds.

In the UK, this began in earnest during the Second World War when domestic food production was stepped up. This set the scene for post-war agriculture, with farmers routinely taking out hedgerows, woodland, ancient forests and specialist flower-rich pastures. These and other unique natural environments, such as wetlands, traditionally sustained a rich and varied insect life as well as birds, small mammals and countless other life forms, from lichens to fungi.

Wild or domesticated grazing animals, sensitively managed, are also vital to the environment, trampling and cropping grassland to allow smaller plant species to flower and fertilizing the soil with their dung (although overgrazing can also be detrimental to the environment).

In the UK, there are some government initiatives underway to try to redress the losses, but the reality is that they are in no way a standalone fix. It would take a massive revolution in food production and agricultural land management to restore our ravaged countryside to meaningful biodiversity. A great many other countries face similar challenges, having allowed modern agricultural practices to fatally deplete their environment. There are parts of China where intense agrichemical use has killed off all bees; without them, farmers now have to pollinate their fruit trees by hand.

Here's another snapshot, showing decades of loss: the 2021 *State of Nature* report from the Royal Society for the Protection of Birds stated, among other things, that 97 per cent of the lowland meadows in England and Wales were lost between the 1930s and 1984 and 80 per cent of the UK's lowland heathland has been destroyed since 1800. Meanwhile, coppiced (i.e. traditionally managed) woodland fell by 90 per cent between 1900 and 1970, and wetlands were drained at a rate of 1,000 square kilometres (386 square miles) per year in the middle of the 19th century.

Compared with honeybees, wild bumblebees and solitaries are even more susceptible to the negative outcomes of modern farming. They are far less numerous, generally less adaptable in their feeding and with shorter flying ranges, meaning they need to live closer to their forage sources. Neither do they have public concern and research focused on them to anything like the same degree as that engine of commerce, the honeybee.

Increasing global urbanization has also contributed to significant loss of biodiversity. Some countries are examining this process more closely, trying to encourage nature to return to towns and cities through 'green' planning. While there have been some significant success stories, far too many governmental and corporate 'green agendas' are patently greenwash, or, at the very least, too little too late. And for every ideal home with its paved driveway, decking on a concrete plinth or an Astroturf lawn, another connection to nature is broken.

There's another, even more complex, factor affecting our pollinators; climate change. For some insect species, such as mosquitoes, global warming represents a great opportunity to extend their territory. For other species it spells disaster. After millions of years of co-evolution between pollinators and plants, their life cycles are powerfully entwined. Many bee species emerge exactly at the point in the year when a primary forage resource begins to flower, and the life of both should proceed in elegant synchronicity.

But when climate change alters the timing of either bee or plant, there's no way back from this ecological mismatch – a phenomenon affecting not only insects, but also birds and many other life forms. The outcome of pollinator mismatch is starvation, leading to unpollinated plants, reduced crop yields and, ultimately, hunger and failure all the way to the human food chain, where we so blithely take continuing supplies for granted.

The global air and sea trade in vegetables and fruit, seeds, plants, animals and bees presents another problem, giving pests and diseases free passage to territories where new hosts have little or no immunity. The natural history of recent centuries is full of the consequences of intentionally or unintentionally relocating living organisms, resulting in the eclipse of, or total loss of, native species.

Please don't despair though. While conservationists all over the world are rightly begging us all to wake up and take notice of species loss, many are also reminding us that we can still act against the decline of the pollinators that underpin our life on this planet. The big important thing – the really big, really important thing – is to plant, or to help plant.

Deeds matter so much more than words. As individuals, we do hold power to make change, whether we exercise that directly through planting, or indirectly through supporting charities and community gardening initiatives. Millions of small interventions add up to something big and meaningful, creating a mosaic of trees, hedges, flower-rich patches and green corridors in which beneficial insects and many interdependent species can find safe haven and thrive.

Millions of tiny interventions can add up to something big and meaningful

CHAPTER 4

25 WILD BEE
Species

25 WILD BEE SPECIES

Welcome to the extraordinary world of bees. Any single species would merit a lifetime of study, but I hope that even the brief profiles included here will charm and intrigue you into looking more closely at these astonishing insects. I've chosen these particular 25 bees partly to give a good cross section of species, but mostly because I just wanted to tell their stories.

Each profile has both similarities and differences, sometimes startling differences, whether it's the Pantaloon Bee with its extravagantly feathery trousers, the Two-coloured Mason Bee, which nests in snail shells, or the Gypsy Cuckoo Bee, which hijacks and enslaves other bees' nests.

To avoid repetition, I've tried to nod at similarities while looking harder either at unique elements of the individual species' life cycle, or at factors that define their family, such as, cellophane bees, which line their nests with a scientifically-baffling substance. The illustrations, too, spotlight the wonderful physical diversity across bee species, rather than forming a field guide.

A QUESTION OF TONGUES

You'll see mention of long and short tongues. Biologically, it's an important distinction. Most solitary bees, as well as honeybees and many bumblebees, have relatively short tongues and depend largely on open-faced or short-tubed flowers. Longer-tongued bees of all species can access much deeper-tubed and more complicated flower forms. A few solitary bees and a fair number of bumblebees benefit from extra-long tongues.

LIFE CYCLE TIMINGS

The months I've quoted relate to the Northern temperate zone, in which the bees featured here are most concentrated. Even within this zone however, timings can vary according to local climate.

WOOL CARDER BEE

*Wool Carders are one of the UK's largest solitary bees. Theirs is a fast
and furious tale of fluff gathering, multiple matings and athletic males using bully-boy
tactics to stake out and defend their perfect patch of flowers against all comers.*

*With their black body and yellow spots sometimes almost forming stripes on the sides
of their abdomen, Wool Carders are easy to recognize but may look like wasps at first
glance. The males (which, unusually, are larger than the females) also have sharp
spines at the end of their abdomen that they use as a weapon.*

♂ *male*

APPROXIMATE SIZE:
Female 11–13 mm (0.43–0.51 in)
Male 14–17 mm (0.55–0.67 in)

SCIENTIFIC NAME:
Anthidium manicatum
FAMILY: *Megachilidae*

WHERE & WHEN YOU'LL SEE THEM

UK density is greater in the south, but
they are present in southern Scotland
as well as in Ireland and the Channel
Islands. Widespread across mainland
Europe, Asia and North Africa, Wool
Carders have also found their way to
New Zealand and the Americas. They
have been called the most widespread
of all non-managed bee species, their
success due to their forage and nesting
adaptability. This makes Wool Carder
Bees an important wild pollinator
species, but they also have the
potential to be an invasive pest.

In late spring and summer, Wool
Carders are often seen in sunny
gardens and a wide range of other
habitats, from fields, meadows
and brownfield sites to paths and
clearings in woodland, and on heaths
and downland. Look for them on
riverbanks too, as well as wetland
areas and even among the vegetation
on shingle beaches.

HABITAT & LIFE CYCLE

The sex life of Wool Carders is intense.
Strong males will claim and mount
a defensive watch over a patch of
flowers, hoping to pounce on and

mate with females arriving to feed. They zip about, defending their patch aggressively from other Wool Carder males and any forage competitors; often honeybees and bumblebees. They employ a range of athletic behaviours to drive insect intruders off, including aerial hovering and wrestling, head-butting and deploying their sharp abdominal spikes to crush and even kill. The better the flowers he has staked out, the more likely a male is to attract females to his patch.

Females mate frequently with different males, and it's all over in seconds. And as seen so often in nature, smaller males that fail to make the grade will hang around waiting to seize a sneaky chance with any passing female.

Once mated, the female builds her nest in an existing small cavity, such as in dead wood, hollow stems, even walls. She lines the nest with fibrous hairs that she has scraped off leaves and stems of woolly plants such as stachys (lamb's ear) with her toothy mandibles (jaws). You can see females flying with woolly bundles in their jaws (and it's these that give this bee the name 'Carder', referencing carding combs traditionally used to tease out tangled sheep's wool).

Back at the nest, the female Wool Carder compresses the woolly masses into individual cells into each of which she deposits an egg and a food parcel to feed the emerging larva. Each parcel combines nectars foraged from a wide variety of flowers and pollen gathered using sticky hairs on the underside of her abdomen. She creates several cells in each nest and, once complete, seals them with a final plug of fibre. She then leaves the nest site forever. Her young emerge the following spring; the males first, to stake out their flower patches, followed some time later by the females.

SUPPORTING THIS BEE

Woolly plants such as stachys and rose campion are essential to these bees, both for forage and nest materials.

Other plantings to feed them could include black horehound, betony, deadnettles, hawksbeard, pelargoniums, great mullein, figwort, mints, purple toadflax, self-heal, yarrow. This list notably includes several members of the *Lamiaceae* (mint) family, a key group for many other bee species. Wool Carder Bees are also fond of leguminous plants including common vetch and bird's-foot trefoil.

Habitat: Leave areas of loose soil bare or create close-mown patches of grass to expose the ground. Hollow stems also appeal (see page 158). Their use of small holes in masonry or timber also makes them candidates for well-managed bee hotels. Plant forage sources close to potential nest sites.

SOLITARY BEES

RED MASON BEE

On a bee expedition in France, we stayed at Château de la Treyne, a venerable hotel in the Dordogne, which that spring had suddenly become a bee hotel too. Masses of Red Masons darted in and out of the building's ancient stone façade and we stood fascinated, working out what they were, and then just watching. Although solitary, these bees are happy to congregate when they find the perfect nesting location and could easily be mistaken for a single colony.

These are among the largest of the Mason Bee species and easiest to identify, with their dense gingery red hair. Males are smaller and slimmer than females with longer antennae and a little patch of white fur on their faces. The Latin name bicornis (two horns) references the two small horns on the female's face, which she uses to help her manipulate mud.

♀ *female*

APPROXIMATE SIZE:
Female 8–10 mm (0.31–0.39 in)
Male 6–8 mm (0.23–0.31 in)

SCIENTIFIC NAME: *Osmia bicornis*
(formerly Osmia rufa)
FAMILY: *Megachilidae*

WHERE & WHEN YOU'LL SEE THEM

Red Mason Bees are common in Britain, with a range including southern England and extending into Scotland, Wales and Ireland. They are also seen in mainland Europe as far north as Sweden and Norway. Further afield, they're found in north Africa, Georgia, Turkey and Iran. One of their close cousins, the Blue Mason Bee (*Osmia caerlescens*) has even wider distribution, adding the Middle East, some parts of India and even the US to its range. (There are eleven different Mason bee species in the UK and 139 in North America.)

Red Masons are happy to nest in the built environment and are well attuned to cultivated garden flowers, but you also see them in wild areas of heathland, moorland and grassland.

Find them in spring and summer. They first emerge in March after developing and hibernating over winter. Laid towards the front of the nest, the males emerge first, with time to build themselves up by feeding while they await the later-emerging females.

There is heated debate among bee experts about which bee pollinators are most effective and Red Masons have a terrific fan base, bristling with facts to prove their superiority over honeybees or bumblebees. Whatever the final count, it's fair to say that Mason Bees are one of the most powerful pollinators in nature.

HABITAT & LIFE CYCLE

Speed is everything in a male Red Mason Bee's agenda. Anticipating the emergence of females, the males mount patrols around the nest, driving off other aspiring males by dive-bombing them. Once females leave the nest, sometimes even before they have fully made it out of the entrance, the males pounce on their backs and begin courtship. Females may reject their advances if they judge a male to be less than desirable, preferring to mate with contenders that have, among other criteria, a strong male odour.
The males die when their work is done.

Mated females immediately start looking for pre-existing holes to serve as nest locations. These can range from cavities in masonry to holes in sandy cliff faces, the interior of plant stems and other small voids. They have also been known to make nests in snail shells and some other odd spots, including keyholes. While Red Mason bees may nest close together in groups, each female works alone.

She begins to construct her nest, first sealing the rear with mud. Mud is vital to these bees and the females 'mine' and transport it using their horns and strong jaws. A single egg is laid in each mud-sealed cell, with female eggs towards the back of the nest and males towards the front, to emerge first. She works hard, visiting a wide range of flowers, and every cell is stocked with its own larder of pollen and nectar to sustain the occupant when the egg hatches into a hungry larva. Later the larvae pupate and overwinter in their cocoons.

Each Red Mason female lays between four and ten eggs in a single nest, and may create four or five separate nests. Once she has sealed a nest with its final stopper of mud, she will not return and dies as the season ends. Her young emerge the following spring.

Red Masons are long-tongued, generalist feeders, gathering pollen and/ or nectar from a wide variety of wild and cultivated plants. Because they emerge around March, they appreciate a good supply of early flowering plants. Reared commercially as well as living wild, they are especially well known as pollinators of orchards and rapeseed.

Trees and bushes: Willow, apple, pear, plum, cherry.

Smaller plants: Borage, crocus, cranesbills, daisies, dandelions, hellebores, lavender and other kitchen herbs, as well as primulas, perennial wallflower, strawberries.

Habitat: Provide dry hollow stems as nest sites (see page 158) and females will also welcome a little muddy patch to help them construct their nests. This species is the best-known candidate for well-managed bee hotels (see page 126).

Dandelions

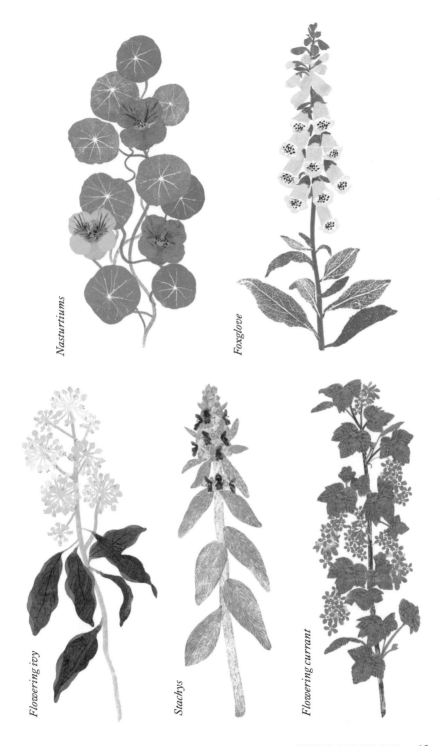

Nasturtiums

Foxglove

Flowering ivy

Stachys

Flowering currant

IVY MINING BEE

Autumn can bring sightings of the Ivy Mining Bee, only recently identified as a distinct species and a relatively new arrival in Britain from mainland Europe. Said to be benefiting from climate change, it was first spotted in Dorset in 2001. Although technically an invasive species, it is not seen as a pest.

At first glance, Ivy Mining Bees look like worker honeybees, but are a little larger, with more clearly defined stripes on their abdomen and a ginger thorax. Since they often forage side by side with honeybees on flowering ivy, you will be able to see the difference.

♀ female

APPROXIMATE SIZE
Female 13 mm (0.51 in)
Male 10 mm (0.39 in)

SCIENTIFIC NAME:: *Colletes hederae*
FAMILY: *Colletidae*

WHERE & WHEN YOU'LL SEE THEM

Ivy Mining Bees are spreading rapidly, not only in Britain (where their range has increased across southern England and into Wales and the Channel Islands) but also across Europe.

They are largely dependent on, and perfectly attuned to, the flowering ivy which produces its alien-looking blooms in autumn. Stopping to take a quiet look at a stand of ivy is your best bet for spotting foraging Ivy Mining Bees. They emerge in late August or September and last sightings can be as late as November.

Females make their nest burrows in cliffs, grassy banks and other urban, country and coastal places with soft, open-textured ground. Although they are solitary bees, each digging their own nest, thousands can congregate in attractive 'nest aggregation' areas, sometimes causing the surrounding soil to collapse.

HABITAT & LIFE CYCLE

The males hatch first, and in particularly large numbers, making competition extraordinarily fierce. They patrol the nesting areas in gangs, so ready to pounce on females that they often jump on each other. This excitement, greatly heightened when a female finally does emerge, creates dramatic clusters of male Ivy Mining Bees. They then have to extricate themselves from the bundle and get back on the prowl, ready to mob the next available female.

Once mated, each female looks for a fairly bare-earth location with soft soil and preferably south facing. Here she digs a burrow with multiple chambers 35–40 cm (14–16 in) underground, into which she lays her eggs. As a member of the Colletidae 'plasterer bee' family, she lines her nest with a cellophane-like waterproof and anti-microbial lining produced from her body and applied with her tongue. One of the lining's key functions is to prevent food stores degenerating over the long period before the adults emerge.

She stores the pollen and nectar she forages as an almost liquid 'soup', ready to feed the larvae when they emerge from the eggs she lays before sealing each cell. Her life cycle lasts roughly six weeks from mating to nesting, foraging, egg laying and nest completion, after which she dies. On their own in the nest, the eggs hatch into larvae, nourished by the pollen stores. They then pupate, to emerge as adult Ivy Mining Bees in late summer of the following year.

Ivy Mining Bees were once thought to live solely on the pollen and nectar of flowering ivy, which is a vital late-season resource for many bees and other insect species. But they have now been observed feeding on other plants, especially if access to flowering ivy is limited.

SUPPORTING THIS BEE

If you plant flowering ivy (*Hedera helix*, also known as English Ivy), it will climb vigorously but take around ten years to become adult and flower. If you already have some, don't cut it back until after the autumn flowering. Ivy's nectar, pollen and berries feed numerous other creatures as well as bees, and its thickets act as valuable shelter for wildlife.

Other plants valuable to Ivy Mining Bees are autumn crocus, bristly ox-tongue, heathers (Erica and Calluna) and goldenrod.

Habitat: If you have a south-facing location with light, soft soil, keep some of it cleared to create bare areas for nest sites. Plant forage sources close by.

SOLITARY BEES

HEATHER COLLETES BEE

In common with its close relatives the Ivy Mining Bee (see page 67) and the Sea Aster Mining Bee, the Heather Colletes is generally associated with a single type of plant, living its life cycle on the same timetable. All three species belong to the genus Colletes, also known as plasterer or cellophane bees because they line their nests with a silky, waterproof, fungus-resistant, cellophane-like coating. They produce it from the Dufour's gland in their abdomen and painstakingly apply it using their unusual forked tongues. Another unusual feature of Colletes bees is the semi-liquid soup of pollen and nectar with which they stock their nest cells (most other bees produce a harder 'bee bread' mixture for their young). Darker than the Ivy Mining Bee, which can also be found foraging on heather, this charming little bee has strongly defined beige and black stripes.

♀ female

APPROXIMATE SIZE:
Female 8.5 mm (0.33 in)
Male 6.5 mm (0.26 in)

SCIENTIFIC NAME:
Colletes succinctus
FAMILY: *Colletidae*

WHERE & WHEN YOU'LL SEE THEM

This is a widespread species seen in Britain as far north as Orkney and west into Wales and southern Ireland. It is also found in the Channel Islands and Scillies. In mainland Europe it runs from Portugal eastwards into Asia as far as Tibet. It is also found in Iran.

Look for this bee from late July to October, on heathland and the ling heather moorland with which it is most closely associated. In mainland Europe, it also populates coastal dunes and beaches. It nests either singly or in large congregations, with each female's nest just a few centimetres away from its neighbours.

These 'nest aggregations', said to be most frequent in the north of Britain, can number tens of thousands of individuals. Finding their own nest in this dense population can be a challenge and they locate it partly by sight, relying on physical landmarks such as a leaf or twig.

The males leave the nest in July/ August to feed and limber up for the slightly later emergence of the females. Patrolling nest areas, they keep watch for emerging females but sometimes end up in a wrestling with other males, rolling around on the ground in a bundle, grappling over a single female.

Once the drama has played out, the mated female digs a short burrow, lining it and creating cell dividers with the 'cellophane' she produces from the Dufours gland in her abdomen. Making foraging trips, she provisions each cell with a fairly liquid mixture of pollen and nectar before laying an egg. Later, the well-fed larvae spin themselves cocoons and wait out the months until they emerge as adults at the end of the following summer.

Females will travel some distance to obtain heather (especially ling heather) pollen for the nest and heather moors can be almost carpeted with foraging bees. If not enough heather is available, Heather Colletes will visit other late-summer forage, including ivy, yarrow and thistles.

SUPPORTING THIS BEE

The three important heathers to plant for this short-tongued bee are ling, bell and cross leaf.

Alongside these, they will welcome creeping thistle, sweet yellow clover, common yarrow, yellow-flowered members of the daisy family and flowering ivy. They will also feed on ragwort, though as this is highly invasive and toxic to many animals, it's best not to plant it.

Habitat: If you live in a heathland or coastal area with loose sandy soil, leave patches bare to attract nesting females to dig burrows. Planting forage close by will also be helpful.

Bell heather

SOLITARY BEES

ASHY MINING BEE

Also known as the Grey Mining Bee, this bee is an engineer, one of the large Andrena family that excavate loose soil and sand. It's obviously a successful nesting strategy, as globally there are more than 1,400 different species of mining bee (with 65 in the UK and 400 in the US alone).

The Ashy Mining Bee is immediately recognizable, with its smart black-and-white colouring. Similar in size to a worker honeybee, the females have a wonderful ruff around the sides of their thorax, contrasting with a glossy black abdomen glinting blue. The males are similar, but smaller and not quite as glamorously arrayed.

♀ *female*

APPROXIMATE SIZE:
Female 10–11 mm (0.30–0.43 in)
Male 9–10 mm (0.35–0.39 in)

SCIENTIFIC NAME::
Andrena cineraria
FAMILY: *Andrena*

WHERE & WHEN YOU'LL SEE THEM

Common in England and the Channel Islands, but rare in Scotland and Ireland, the Ashy Mining Bee is well established across central Europe and Scandinavia and east into China. It's on the wing from late March until June or even July.

Females can be seen scoping out nest sites from late March and they are surprisingly adaptable. You may spot them by the coast, in short grass and cliffs, or on heath and downland as well as on the margins of moors and open woodland. They also populate brownfield sites and other human-made spaces, including path edges, quarries and gardens – anywhere sunny, with a soft, sandy soil and good forage within easy reach. Liking bare earth or short grazed or mown grass, this is one of the bee species that may decide to take up residence in your lawn.

HABITAT & LIFE CYCLE

As the just-hatched females leave the nest for the first time, they are grabbed by males that have been madly zipping around the site since emerging a few days earlier. Newly mated, each female finds herself a nest site, ideally south facing, either isolated or amongst an aggregation of individual Ashy Mining Bee nests.

She digs in the friable soil, using her strong jaws to break it up and her legs to sweep it away. Gradually tunnelling in, she engineers a main nest tunnel branching into several chambers.

Foraging hard, flying between her chosen flowers and the nest site, the female stocks each chamber with nectar-moistened pollen. She must defend her nest too, as the stored food can attract would-be robbers, or cuckoo species hoping to lay their eggs in her prepared space. Looking like a little volcano, the nest can be sealed with loose soil to defend the tunnel entrance against incomers or bad weather.

The female lays a single egg in each chamber and seals it in, and that is the end of her maternal duty. The eggs hatch into larvae that will feast on the pollen stores before spinning their cocoons to overwinter. They will emerge as adults the following year.

SUPPORTING THIS BEE

Ashy Mining Bees gather pollen and/ or nectar from a fairly wide variety of plants, including:

Trees and bushes: Fruit trees and bushes of all sorts, including apple, blackcurrants, brambles/blackberry, cherry, blackthorn, ceanothus, gorse, hawthorn, willows.

Smaller plants: Bluebells, buttercups (*Ranunculus acris* and others), daisies, dandelions, euphorbia/spurge, oilseed rape, thrift and many umbelliferae (the carrot family, which includes cow parsley, angelica, parsnips, dill and many others).

Habitat: Leave areas of soft, preferably sandy, soil bare and create some close-mown patches of grass to mimic grazed land. Plant forage sources close to potential nesting sites.

Gorse

TAWNY MINING BEE

The female Tawny Mining Bee is a glamorous creature, vivid in her thick, foxy-red furry coat with a jet-black face, underside and legs. Mining bees like these often dig their burrows in short grass. This is a good reason to keep some areas of lawn mown, effectively to mimic grazed pastureland. Male Tawny Mining Bees lack the showiness of the females. They are slimmer, still gingery but far less furry and less brightly coloured. They do have a smart white tuft on their faces, though, which is a good way of identifying them.

♀ *female*

APPROXIMATE SIZE
Female 10–12 mm (0.39–0.44 in)
Male 8–10 mm (0.23–0.39 in)

SCIENTIFIC NAME: *Andrena fulva*
FAMILY: *Andrenidae*

WHERE & WHEN YOU'LL SEE THEM

From March to June, these bees occur throughout most of southern Britain and extend up into north and central Scotland, as well as Ireland and the Channel Islands. Eastwards they occur across Europe to the Balkans and southwards into southern Scandinavia.

Although widely geographically distributed, they have a low population density, so may not be that easy to find. On the plus side, they feed from a large variety of different flowers and occupy both urban and rural habitats, so it's always worth keeping an eye out for that flash of vivid ginger. This is a bee you may well encounter in a city park.

HABITAT & LIFE CYCLE

The life cycle of the Tawny Mining Bee is set to coincide with the flowering of major fruit trees such as apples. They pollinate the trees as they move from flower to flower gathering nectar and pollen.

After emerging from the overwintered nest, the young males spend their time feeding and keeping a close eye on the nest site. Running patrols, they wait for hatched out females to leave the nest, triggering intense competition to mate.

Once mated, the female has only a few short weeks of life to find a place to mine a burrow and lay her eggs. She's searching for a south-facing site with short grass or sparse vegetation and soft soil in which she can easily undertake her earthworks. Digging with her jaws and brushing loose soil away with her legs, she can rapidly tunnel down vertically around 20–30 cm (8–12 in), building chambers off the main shaft. She provisions each one with pollen and a little nectar before laying a single egg, sealing it up and moving on to set up the next one. Once the entire nest is completed, still early in the summer, she leaves it and dies shortly afterwards. Her eggs hatch after just a few days and then pupate over winter, emerging as adult bees the following spring.

Whether in a flower bed, a sunny bank, mown grass or sparsely vegetated margins, the tiny holes drilled by mining bees look like small volcanoes, with a heap of earth piled up at the entrance. You might see them singly or in aggregations (clusters of solitary nests). Mining bees often get blamed for creating bare patches in lawns, but in fact have simply chosen that bare earth as a good place to dig their burrow.

The parasitic Bee Fly (*Bombylius major*, see page 38) is fond of placing its eggs in Tawny Mining bee nests.

SUPPORTING THIS BEE

Tawny Mining Bees are short-tongued but gather pollen and/or nectar from a wide variety of plants, including:

Trees and bushes: Apple, beech, blackthorn, cherry, gooseberry, hawthorn, holly, maple, oak, pear, plum, sycamore, willow, wayfaring tree.

Smaller plants: Buttercup, lawn/common daisy, daffodil, dandelion, garlic mustard, oilseed rape.

Habitat: Leave areas of soft, preferably sandy, soil bare or create some close-mown patches of grass in sunny south-facing spots.

Crab apple

TWO-COLOURED MASON BEE

This bee is unique in nesting exclusively in empty snail shells. Not every shell suits the purpose and wherever they are geographically located, Two-coloured Mason Bees (also known as Red-tailed Mason Bees) are associated with specific snail species. Although not rare across its whole territory, this bee is classified as 'notable' in the UK.

It's not only the females who seek out snail shells. Males have also been spotted inside empty shells, using them as a shelter from cold or wet weather and as a safe place to spend the night. They will defend these shells quite strongly.

♀ *female*

APPROXIMATE SIZE:
Female 8–10 mm (0.31–0.39 in)
Males 7–9 mm (0.27–0.35 in)

SCIENTIFIC NAME:: *Osmia bicolor*
FAMILY: *Megachilidae*

WHERE & WHEN YOU'LL SEE THEM

From southern mainland Britain, including south Wales, Two-coloured Mason Bee territory extends north as far as southern Scandinavia, eastwards to Central Asia and south into Italy, Spain and Romania.

They populate the calcium-rich landscapes that support their allied snail species (snail shells being made from calcium) plus woodland, heath and grassland with limestone and chalk soils. Quarries and brownfield sites can also fit the bill.

This is an early-emerging bee, with males active in March or even February. But generally, April to July is the time to see this species foraging, or, if you are incredibly lucky, inspecting their precious snail shells.

HABITAT & LIFE CYCLE

The male bees emerge a couple of weeks before the females, building up strength to swoop on and mate with the young females when they leave the nesting site. During its brief lifetime, a male mates up to seven times before exhausting its supply of sperm.

A mated female will begin finding and inspecting empty snail shells, turning them over to have a good look. She builds several separate nests in different shells over the course of her brief lifetime.

Smaller shells can host just a single egg, while larger ones accommodate up to five. Each cell is provisioned with balls of pollen and nectar created by the female, on top of which she lays the egg. The cells are partitioned with leaves chewed into a building material by the female. The nest is vulnerable to predation while the female is out foraging, so she makes each trip as quick as possible by collecting pollen from a single plant type.

Ultimately, the female seals the shell with the same chewed-leaf material, also smearing it over the outside of the shell as camouflage. As another security measure against predators, she places a gritty barrier of sand or soil between the last cell and the final plug. She also rotates the shell to leave it face down in the soil or even partially buried. Finally, she builds another layer of camouflage, creating a little shelter of woodland litter – including twigs, dead leaves and grass – that she has picked and flown back to the nest. She glues these finds together with saliva, creating a rudimentary roof.

SUPPORTING THIS BEE

Two-coloured Mason Bees are long-tongued and can forage widely, but females tend to gather pollen from a single source to make their collecting trips as quick and productive as possible. These are some of the plants that they have been reported as visiting:

Trees and bushes: Blackthorn, gorse, oak, willow, maple.

Smaller plants: Bluebells, bird's-foot-trefoil, daisies, dandelion, heath dog violet, ground-ivy, horseshoe vetch, sainfoin, wood anemone.

Habitat: If you live in an area with limestone or chalk soil, pick up empty snail shells you find and place them at the back of your flower beds, close to forage resources. Hopefully, a female Two-coloured Mason Bee will give them consideration, or a male will use them as shelter.

Wood anemone

VIOLET CARPENTER BEE

Derived from the Greek, Xylocopa means woodworker and although it is so rare in Britain, this giant carpentry expert is my absolute favourite bee. Despite being relatively new to the UK, it is widespread in mainland Europe and my first encounter was in Italy, where I was drawn over to a stand of flowers by inordinately noisy buzzing and waves of disruption among the plants. What I first assumed to be an enormous flying beetle turned out to be a Violet Carpenter, the largest, most beautiful bee I'd ever seen.

First seen in Britain in 2006, probably having arrived from Europe in a consignment of timber or plants, the Violet Carpenter Bee has been slowly but steadily increasing its range, taking advantage of climate change. This is a breathtaking bee to encounter, both for its size and for its gleaming black body with iridescent purple glints. Its wings also have a metallic lustre. It is among the largest bees in Europe.

♀ *female*

APPROXIMATE SIZE
Female 20–30 mm (0.79–1.18 in)
Male 20–30 mm (0.79–1.18 in)

SCIENTIFIC NAME: *Xylocopa violacea*
FAMILY: *Apidae*

WHERE & WHEN YOU'LL SEE THEM

From their native territory around the Mediterranean and the Black Sea, Violet Carpenter Bees have spread into northern Europe, including Poland, Belgium and Germany. In Britain the species was first sighted in Wales in 2006 and Leicestershire in 2007. It has since been seen in the Midlands, Yorkshire, Wales and the Channel Islands. Although some sightings may be of 'vagrants' (chance visitors), it seems likely to be naturalizing.

Further afield, its range goes east across Europe into central China and it is also found in some northern parts of India. These bees are on the wing from April until June, although early-emerging males can sometimes be seen early in March. Not surprisingly, being carpenter bees, they are woodland margin dwellers.

In spring, mated females go in search of nest sites. Equipped with powerful jaws, they tunnel into soft, rotten or even sound wood, either in trees or bushes or in structural elements in the built environment. (Where there is no suitable wood, large diameter hollow plant stems are the next best thing.)

Wood tunnelling is common among carpenter bee species and leads to some people seeing them as disruptive pests, although they are also acknowledged as valuable crop pollinators, especially as, like bumblebees, they can buzz pollinate. The female bee creates a main tunnel, sometimes adding smaller branch tunnels. Using those incredible jaws, she then bites off and chews wood into a form of paper with which she can build thick cell partition walls. The nest will contain just seven or eight eggs in total, each in its own cell, stocked with pollen and nectar and then sealed. Female Violet Carpenters are highly defensive while they build their nests, using continuous buzzing, rushing towards the entrance and even taking to the air to repel nest site predators or competitors.

The Violet Carpenter Bee belongs to the *Xylocopa* genus. Some *Xylocopa* species are known to be primitively social, with founding females guarding their young as they hatch into larvae and then pupate. The young adults emerge in autumn and are sometimes fed by the founding female and spend the winter in the parental nest, leaving the following spring to build their own nests. However, it not clear whether this is the case with this bee. It is still most often described as following the usual pattern of a solitary female building her own nest and leaving it sealed for her offspring to mature without her. But some research sources offer tantalizing wisps of commentary disputing this, suggesting that Violet Carpenters may be social to varying degrees as population density, forage and climate allow.

SUPPORTING THIS BEE

Violet Carpenter Bees are fairly short tongued. They gather widely from flowers of many different families but, like so many other bee species, are said to be fond of plants in the *Fabaceae* (pea/bean) and *Lamiaceae* (mint/sage/dead-nettle) families. Like honeybees and some bumblebees, they show floral fidelity (generally foraging on a single type of flower at a time). Here are some other plants specifically reported as Violet Carpenter forage sources:

Trees and bushes: Wisteria, fruit trees, especially peaches.

Smaller plants: Broad/fava beans, runner beans, lavenders, mints, nasturtiums (*Tropaeolum spp./Tropaeolum majus*), scorpion senna.

PANTALOON BEE

Who could resist wanting to know more about this wondrously named creature? Even its Latin name, Dasypoda hirtipes, is entrancing. Rather less romantically though, it is also known as the Hairy-legged Mining Bee.

Both sexes are golden brown and black striped, but the 'pantaloons' in question belong only to the female. Her hind legs are almost feathery, covered with long, tawny-coloured hairs. As she visits flowers, pollen sticks to the hairs, building up progressively to a rather spectacular pair of knickerbockers. The males are also hairy, but lack the pantaloons and their hair fades in the sun, leaving them a silvery-white.

♀ *female*

APPROXIMATE SIZE:
Male and female 10–11 mm (0.39–0.43 in)

SCIENTIFIC NAME:
Dasypoda hirtipes
FAMILY: *Melittidae*

WHERE & WHEN YOU'LL SEE THEM

In Britain Pantaloon Bees are rare, living in heathland and sandy coastal areas, generally in the southeast but ranging from Norfolk to west Wales and the Channel Islands, with scattered sightings elsewhere. But they are widespread in global terms, found across Europe, including southern Scandinavia and through into China and Russia's Far East. They are also found in north Africa.

In Europe, you'll see them mainly between June and late August, and because they feed principally on plants in the daisy family (*Asteraceae*), having a strong preference for those with yellow flowers, these can give a good steer in looking for them. They are also said to do most of their foraging in the morning.

HABITAT & LIFE CYCLE

The exposed sandy areas that these mining bees seek out occur in a variety of places, in both town and country. Their ideal locations are south-facing dunes, cliffs and heaths. Loose sand makes it easy for them to dig their burrows but they will also nest in salt marshes and sparse, scrubby grassland.

As usual with solitary bees, the males emerge first from the overwintered nest. They spend time conditioning themselves, feeding and flying, getting ready to mate when the females emerge a little later.

Mated females dig deep underground burrows, sometimes as long as 90 cm (3 ft). They excavate at an angle, using their pantaloon legs as they work, reversing out of the nest with their furry hind legs extended to push the soil along like a snow plough. This creates a fan of loose soil outside the nest, very different from the volcano-like mounds created by many other mining bee species.

These are solitary bees, but numerous females can build their nests in proximity. In the 1960s, scientists reported an aggregation of around 7.65 million nests on the banks of the Barysh river in Russia's southern Ulyanovsk region.

In each cell of their nest, female Pantaloons build what is described as a 'tripod-like' structure topped with a ball of nectar-moistened pollen stores and an egg. Unusually, their larvae do not spin themselves cocoons. Growing to adulthood in the nest that the female has sealed and left, they emerge the following spring to begin the life cycle again.

SUPPORTING THIS BEE

Pantaloon Bees are short-tongued and forage on wildflowers, principally in the daisy (*Asteracea*) family. They especially like those with yellow flowers, as well as many wild and cultivated thistles.

Plants to attract them include cat's ear, common fleabane, sow thistle, hawkbit, hawk's beard, knapweeds, spear thistle and bristly ox-tongue. Ragworts are also very attractive to these bees, but not recommended to plant as they are highly invasive and toxic to many animals.

Habitat: If your garden has a loose, sandy soil, leave a sunny, south-facing area bare for burrowing bees.

Common knapweed

SMALL SCISSOR BEE

Slim with large heads and shiny black bodies, Small Scissor Bees could, at first glance, seem to be flies or winged ants. But their anatomy and very specific foraging behaviour will help you identify them as little bees. Although males and females are the same size and similarly coloured, the female has white hairs on the underside of her abdomen, designed for collecting pollen.

The male also has a distinctive feature – a double pronged 'peg' on the last segment of his abdomen. He uses this to grip onto flowers, either when resting in them at night or when sheltering from bad weather.

♀ *female*

APPROXIMATE SIZE
Male and female 4–4.5 mm (0.15–0.17 in)

SCIENTIFIC NAME:
Chelostoma campanularum
FAMILY: *Megachilidae*

WHERE & WHEN YOU'LL SEE THEM

Living in south and central England, Small Scissor Bees also have a geographical spread across Europe, into North Africa and Asia. Introduced to North America in the 1960s, populations are recorded on the east coast of the USA, in Upper New York State and in Connecticut and northwards into Canada.

As another common name 'Harebell Carpenter Bee' suggests, they depend almost exclusively on campanulas (bellflower species) for forage and shelter. You'll see these bees between June and August feeding on cultivated garden campanulas and wild ones on heath and downland.

HABITAT & LIFE CYCLE

Emerging first from the nest, young males feed, shelter and even sleep in campanula flowers. The later-emerging females head for the same patches to feed and mate.

Nest locations chosen by mated females (usually tiny holes in timber, already bored out by a woodworm or beetle) will, again, be close to campanulas.

Their nests have partitions constructed from soil, nectar and saliva, each cell provisioned with pollen & nectar collected before laying an egg and sealing it in. The Latin name *Chelostoma* means clawed mouth. The female clings to the anthers of the flower with her strong jaws and front legs, securing herself while she uses her back legs to brush pollen onto the hairy underside of her abdomen.

Once the nest is completed and sealed up with a final plug of sand and small pebbles, the female dies shortly afterwards. The next generation will hatch, pupate and emerge as adults the following year.

SUPPORTING THIS BEE

This bee needs bellflowers for both food and shelter and it's helpful to plant them. There are masses of species to choose from, including peach-leaved bellflower, harebells (*C. rotundifolia*, sometimes known as Scottish bluebells), Canterbury bells, nettle-leaved bellflower, rampions, clustered bellflower, Carpathian bellflower and sheep's bit scabious.

Habitat: Although keen on nesting in old insect borings, Small Scissor Bees have also been known to use hollow plant stems (see page 158) and may also be candidates for well-maintained bee hotels (see page 126).

Campanula

SOLITARY BEES

PATCHWORK LEAFCUTTER BEE

If you catch sight of a flying bee apparently transporting a section of leaf, you're not imagining things – you've just seen a Leafcutter Bee at work, carrying nest material that she's painstakingly bitten off. There are seven species of Leafcutter Bee in the UK, of which the Patchwork Leafcutter is one of the most common, along with Willughby's Leafcutter Bee (Megachile willughbiella).

Roughly the size of a honeybee, but more squat in form, females have orange hairs on the underside of their abdomen, often said to look like a bright halo. These hairs are highly efficient pollen traps, making this bee a very effective pollinator. Males are slimmer, with a fluffier appearance but without the orange abdominal hairs.

♀ *female*

APPROXIMATE SIZE:
Female 9–13 mm (0.35–0.51 in)
Male 8-12 mm (0.31 – 0.47 in)

SCIENTIFIC NAME:
Megachile centuncularis
FAMILY: *Megachilidae*

WHERE & WHEN YOU'LL SEE THEM

Fairly common, the Patchwork Leafcutter lives across Britain, from the south right up to the north of Scotland and eastern Ireland, as well as the Channel Islands. Globally, it's found across Europe and into Asia as well as coast to coast in Canada and in the US's northern states.

Spot this bee from mid June until the beginning of September. An adaptable nester and forager, it nests in both the countryside and urban gardens. If you see circular or oval 'bites' cut out of leaves on rose bushes, honeysuckles, lilacs, horse chestnuts, birches or ash trees, it will likely be the work of Leafcutters.

HABITAT & LIFE CYCLE

Newly hatched males feed and patrol the nest area, ready to jump on females as soon as they emerge. Once the female has mated, she starts to hunt for her own nest site.

Patchwork Leafcutters are resourceful, happy to build anywhere from holes in wood or walls to hollow plant stems. They will even nest directly in soil. The female uses her jaws like a pair of scissors, neatly cutting out disc sections of leaves and flying them back to her nest. There she uses her legs to roll them up, creating small packages or cells, each of which she provisions with foraged pollen and nectar, before laying a single egg and sealing it up.

Observers have noted Patchwork Leafcutters employing between six and 14 pieces of leaf to build each cell and a further six or seven discs to create a divider. Once finished, they complete the nest entrance with a seal made from yet more leaf discs.

The progeny overwinter in their leafy cells, finally metamorphosing into adults and emerging the following spring. As with almost all solitary bees, the male eggs are laid in the last few cells, allowing them to emerge from the nest before the females. The fact that the youngest bees hatch first is one of the peculiarities of linear-nesting solitary bees.

SUPPORTING THIS BEE

Patchwork Leafcutters are long-tongued bees, gathering pollen and/ or nectar from a wide variety of plants, some of which also provide the leaves they use in nesting. Brambles and thistles are often noted as favourite foraging sources.

Trees and bushes: Ash, birch, horse chestnut, lilac, roses, honeysuckle, snowberry, brambles.

Smaller plants: Alkanet, baptisia, buttercups, cornflower, burdock, dandelion, black-eyed Susan, goldenrod, thistles.

Habitat: Don't cut your hollow-stemmed plants to the ground at the end of the flowering season. Just trim the plants back, leaving lengths of cut stem standing to provide natural nest sites for the following year's bees. Site forage and leaf-providing plants nearby. These bees may also nest in well-managed bee hotels (see page 126).

Dog rose

SOLITARY BEES

COMMON FURROW BEE

Change and adaptation are vital in evolution and Common Furrow Bees, plus several other related species, are particularly fascinating because they exhibit social polymorphism. This means that they show both solitary and socially organized life cycles within the same species, and even switch between the two. This offers scientists unique research opportunities.

Also known as the Slender Mining Bee, the Common Furrow Bee is in the genus commonly known as 'Sweat Bees', because of their need for sodium (salt). In coastal regions they obtain it by licking flowers, but the search for salt can also attract them to lick hot, sweaty humans. They have developed a tongue ideal for licking, referenced in the genus's more formal name of Lasioglossum, which means hairy tongue.

♂ male

APPROXIMATE SIZE:
Male and female 5–7 mm (0.19–0.28 in)

SCIENTIFIC NAME:
Lasioglossum calceatum
FAMILY: *Halictidae*

WHERE & WHEN YOU'LL SEE THEM

This important pollinator found throughout Britain, as far as northern Scotland, the Scilly Isles, Channel Islands, Isle of Man and parts of Ireland. In mainland Europe they extend as far north as Finland, moving southerly across the continent into Turkey (often in mountainous areas) and to east Asia, including North Korea, the Russian Far East, China and Japan.

From April to October, they are on the wing in a wide range of different urban and countryside locations. They can also nest at altitudes of up to 1,800 m (5,900 ft).

HABITAT & LIFE CYCLE

This is where things get really interesting. As early as 1972, Japanese researchers found two types of Common Furrow Bee behaviour – solitary nesting in higher, cooler areas and social colonial nesting in more hospitable lowlands where the spring/summer season was long enough to allow two generations to be raised in a single year. Studies in other countries have confirmed this, reporting that social Common Furrow bees revert to solitary nesting when relocated to cooler terrain. This bee and related species such as the Orange-legged Furrow Bee (widely studied in the USA) give scientists real insights into the genesis of social adaptation.

Social bees' caste system is seen clearly in honeybees and bumblebees, and even in the more primitively social Common Furrow Bee, in which the female founding the nest dominates as a queen. Her brood first consists of female workers that take over the foraging and help rear a 'reproductive' generation of males and females. Mated females then overwinter alone.

Social or solitary, Common Furrow Bees like to nest in open, sunny situations such as short turf or even bare earth. Here, nest-founding females dig vertical burrows with branch tunnels leading to nest chambers where brood cells are built and provisioned with pollen moistened with nectar to sustain the larvae on their journey to adulthood.

SUPPORTING THIS BEE

Common Furrow Bees forage widely, but are known to favour the aster family including black-eyed Susan, dandelions, echinacea (coneflowers), goldenrod, knapweed, liatris, thistles and sunflowers. Plants from other families on which they have been recorded feeding include hardy geraniums and, in the US, purple meadow rue, daisies of all sorts (*Asteraceae*), knapweed, liatris, thistles and sunflowers.

Habitat: Leave areas of clear soil or short turf in sunny areas to offer them nesting grounds and plant forage sources close by.

Wild geranium

LONG-HORNED BEE

This handsome solitary bee was once widespread in southern Britain. Largely due to habitat loss, it has now become rare and is considered one of Britain's most declined species.

Extremely long, elegantly curved antennae make the males immediately recognizable. Females are a similar size but slightly sturdier. They share the male's light golden-brown thorax and abdomen, but sadly not those splendid long 'horns'.

♂ *male*

APPROXIMATE SIZE:
Male and female 13 mm (0.51 in)

SCIENTIFIC NAME:
Eucera longicornis
FAMILY: *Apidea*

WHERE & WHEN YOU'LL SEE THEM

Males emerge in mid-May. The females appear a couple of weeks later and can be seen foraging until July/August.

The global range of this bee runs across western Europe, south into Mediterranean areas and east into Siberia and China. It is extremely susceptible to loss of forage and nesting habitat, especially caused by industrialized farming and coastal erosion. This has become acute in Britain, where the Long-horned Bee is now rare, seen only on around a dozen coastal sites in southern England and Wales.

HABITAT & LIFE CYCLE

Leaving the nest in spring and waiting for the females to emerge a little later, male Long-horned Bees become so keen to mate that they can be fooled by the charms of a flower, the bee orchid (*Ophrys apifera*, especially widespread in Mediterranean regions). Not only does this flower mimic the physical appearance of a female bee, it also gives out an alluring perfume, fooling male Long-horned Bees (and a couple of other bee species) into trying to mate with it. This sexual mimicry by the plant is a clever tactic to achieve cross-pollination.

Generally, though, the males get it right and female Long Horns are mated as soon as they leave the nest. Each female then explores areas of bare, sparsely vegetated, grazed or eroded soil where she can excavate her burrow. Although solitary, she may join an aggregation of Long-horned females settling in the same territory. Other priorities are a south-facing site and plentiful forage nearby, particularly wildflowers native to the habitats that the species favours.

Having dug a burrow, the female smooths its walls and starts to build cells, provisioning each with a pollen and honey paste, on top of which she lays an egg before sealing the cell and moving on to build the next one. Eventually, sealing the nest, she leaves and dies soon afterwards. Her brood will mature on its own and emerge the following spring.

SUPPORTING THIS BEE

The Long-horned Bee is now so rare that few people will realistically be able to encourage them in their area. But if you are in, or close to, an area where they do still exist, planting to increase their forage is a great thing to do. And remember that anything you plant in hope of attracting Long Horns will also be hugely valuable to other pollinators.

Long-horned Bees have a special preference for members of the *Fabaceae* (pea family), particularly any of the vetches, including kidney vetch and meadow vetchling, as well as clovers, bird's-foot trefoil and sweet peas. They also enjoy bugle, brambles/blackberry, comfrey, heather and ground-ivy.

If you do live in or near one of their remaining territories, you could also join a local nature society to raise awareness, encourage others to plant close to where nest sites have been identified and defend against agrichemical use in that area.

Habitat: You could leave some places where their wild forage plants grow unmown from mid-April to mid-July and keep nest areas of bare(ish) ground clear of invasive vegetation from May until August.

Meadow vetchling

SOLITARY BEES

COMMON YELLOW-FACED BEE

There are 11 species of Yellow-faced Bee found in the British Isles alone and well over 100 species in the USA. They are rare in having no pollen-collecting features on their bodies. Instead, they eat nectar and pollen, storing it inside their bodies in pouches (crops) to regurgitate when they return to the nest.

This species' scientific name communis refers to its extremely widespread nature. Much of its success lies in its incredible adaptability as to where it lives and which flowers it visits.

Yellow-faced Bees are all small and slightly waspy-looking, with black bodies and yellow masks. In this particular species, the male has a prominent triangular yellow facial marking. The female's mask is often smaller.

♂ *male*

APPROXIMATE SIZE:
Male and female 4.5–6 mm (0.18–0.23 in)

SCIENTIFIC NAME:
Hylaeus communis
FAMILY: *Colletidae*

WHERE & WHEN YOU'LL SEE THEM

With territories including coastal, lowland and mountainous areas, this bee is widespread across much of Britain, running north into central Scotland and west to eastern Ireland. Across Europe, its northerly range extends up past the Arctic Circle and southerly into Lebanon and northern Iran. It is also reported as a 'new exotic' in the USA and Canada.

Flying from May to September, these tiny bees work an extraordinary range of habitats and flowers. Places you might see them include bramble bushes, gravel pits, woodlands, uparks and gardens and rewilding brownfield sites.

HABITAT & LIFE CYCLE

Once females have emerged from the nest, encountered the already-active males and mated, they begin scoping out the ideal nest site. Unlike many species, they have a wide range of options, although generally preferring to nest off the ground. Highly opportunistic, they repurpose existing cavities, happy to build their nests in abandoned insect-bored tunnels, cracks in plaster or mortar, or hollow plant stalks (their jaws are not strong enough to dig their own tunnels).

As a member of the *Colletidae* family (the plasterers/cellophane bees), the female lines her nest with a near-magical substance that she secretes and paints on with her tongue. It's an ultra-thin cellophane/silk that's waterproof and gives protection against fungi and bacteria. Scientist are fascinated by this durable gossamer material, which can withstand even strong chemicals applied in laboratory tests. There is an astonishing YouTube video showing a Yellow-faced Bee creating and manipulating the cellophane (search 'Common Yellow-faced bee making its cellophane-like nest'). Providing each cell with a soup of pollen and nectar before laying an egg and sealing it off, she finally completes the nest, creates a final seal and leaves.

If climate and forage availability permit, a first generation of adults may emerge from the nest in August in time for those females to mate, nest and lay a second generation that will then overwinter.

SUPPORTING THIS BEE

The Common Yellow-faced Bee is short-tongued, but, being small, is able to access many different floral sources. Specific foraging observations include:

Allium species (including chives, round headed leek, leek, onion), autumn hawkbit, goldenrod, ground elder, harebells, mignonette, purple loosestrife, Queen Anne's lace, red hemp nettle, tansy, thistles (including creeping thistle and spear thistle), sedum (stonecrop/*Sedum*), vipers' bugloss, charlock/wild mustard, yarrow.

Habitat: The ideal diameter for Common Yellow-faced Bees' nesting sites is a 3-mm (0.11-in) hole. This means it could be housed in a well-managed bee hotel. Alternatively, leave slim, hollow stalks in the garden as nest sites and/or mimic beetle borings by drilling 3-mm holes in wooden posts or logs in a wildlife woodpile.

Viper's bugloss

SOLITARY BEES

HAIRY-FOOTED FLOWER BEE

Flower Bees (also known as Common Fur Bees) are a group of solitaries belonging to the Apidae, the largest bee family of all, numbering around 6,000 species including all honeybees, bumblebees and stingless bees. This highlights the incredible diversity of specialisms within the bee world. Largely unknown to most people, thousands upon thousands of wild bee species quietly live their lives, pollinating plant species and forging links in the food chains of millions of other living organisms.

♂ *male*

APPROXIMATE SIZE
*Male and female 13–15 mm
(0.51–0.59 in)*

SCIENTIFIC NAME::
Anthophora plumipes
FAMILY: *Apidae*

WHERE & WHEN YOU'LL SEE THEM

Male Hairy-footed Flower Bees are natural dandies, pairing a dense gingery pelt with elaborately feathered legs designed to attract females. Their middle legs are elongated to emphasize the effect and a patch of cream fur on their faces completes the look. Less extravagantly feathery, but still densely furred, females are usually black with reddish-ginger legs showing prominent pollen brushes on the rear set. Being so furry (they're often mistaken for bumblebees), both sexes are excellent pollinators, trapping pollen on their entire body.

Woodlands and urban green spaces are equally popular with this bee. Males emerge early, in March or sometimes even February. Look for them especially on patches of lungwort. Females emerge a couple of weeks later and can be seen until June.

Hairy-footed Flower Bees are common in south-eastern England and Wales. They are also reported in northern England and Scotland and have recently been seen for the first time in Ireland. Most of Europe has them too, as does north Africa and parts of Asia, including China and Japan. They were introduced to the USA in the 1980s and are prospering in Washington DC and Maryland.

Although they look a bit like bumblebees, the males have a very different, high-pitched, buzz, with a zippy way of flying and an ability to hover shared by the foraging females. You'll find males vigorously defending patches of flowers (especially lungwort) against all comers, and rapidly patrolling nest sites at close quarters as they wait for the females to come out. They then hover behind the females to pounce and attempt to mate, all the while displaying their fine leg feathers.

The mated female will hunt for a place where she can excavate a nest, which may be part of an aggregation, with masses of Hairy-footed Flower Bees nesting close together. These large groups are said to be fairly noisy.

Mud and clay walls and banks of bare earth on south-facing sites are all attractive, as are crumbly cliff faces or softened mortar. Traditional 'cob' (essentially mud and straw) bricks are always mentioned as ideal nesting sites for these bees. They have also been recorded ground nesting in compacted clay soil.

Nest construction proceeds with the female building a series of cells, each provisioned with a mass of pollen and nectar, crowned by an egg and then sealed. The final mud seal to secure the nest may be built using water imported in batches to soften the soil, which she then literally licks into shape using her tongue and body. (There is a wonderful video of this work on YouTube – search '*Anthophora plumipes* Hairy-footed Flower Bee sealing nest'). Her nest building completed, the female dies, leaving her brood to emerge early the following spring.

SUPPORTING THIS BEE

Quite unusually for solitary bees, Hairy-footed Flower Bees have a long tongue, enabling them to feed from deep-tubed flowers. Again unusually, they forage up to 4 km (2½ miles) from their nest site. Above all, plant lungwort, as well as other spring flowers such as primroses, comfrey and red, spotted and white deadnettles.

Other plants they enjoy include aubrieta, azaleas, borage, daffodils, gorse, herb robert, rosemary, violets and wallflowers.

Habitat: Leave soft mortar joints in brick or stone buildings if it doesn't compromise the structure. Soft cob bricks also attract these bees. If you have space, leave some soil bare in a sunny area of the garden. South-facing banks are ideal too, either planted with lungwort or primroses or mown very short (as if grazed) so that the soil is exposed as a potential nesting site.

COMMON MOURNING BEE

This unforgettably named solitary species is a cleptoparasite (clepto from the Greek/ Latin 'to steal') that preys on Anthophora, or flower bees, especially the Hairy-footed Flower Bee (see page 90). The life cycles of these insects are inextricably linked – as are those of many other bee species with the cuckoo bees and other parasites that exploit them.

You can't mistake this bee, with its pitch-black body and distinctive white spots along the sides of its abdomen. Females are slightly larger than males, which also have white hairs on their head and thorax. In the UK, a very similar bee, the Square-Spotted Mourning Bee, is now thought to be extinct, having declined in parallel with its key host, the Potter Flower Bee.

♀ *female*

APPROXIMATE SIZE
*Male and female: 10–13 mm
(0.39–0.51 in)*

SCIENTIFIC NAME:
Melecta albifrons
FAMILY: *Apidae*

WHERE & WHEN YOU'LL SEE THEM

From March to June, Common Mourning Bees haunt locations where Hairy-footed Flower Bees are nesting en masse, from crumbly cliff faces to urban parks and gardens.

Although they don't live in anything like the same density as their hosts, in the UK they tend to be found from the Midlands down to the south and into the Channel Islands. As the Hairy-footed Flower Bee extends its range northwards into Yorkshire and Scotland, so does the Common Mourning Bee. Globally, its recorded range mirrors that of flower bees, occupying much of Europe, north Africa and the Middle East into Iran.

HABITAT & LIFE CYCLE

Mated Common Mourning Bee females deliberately overfly flower bee nest aggregations, watching and waiting for opportunities to sneak in.

As a flower bee female flies out to go foraging, the parasitic Mourning Bee snatches her moment to enter the nest. Piercing the seal on a cell, she lays her own egg alongside that of the flower bee egg and its painstakingly gathered stocks of pollen and nectar.

When the Common Mourning Bee's eggs hatch into larvae, they immediately eat their cell mate, the host's egg or larvae. Now solo, the Mourning Bee larva grows fat on the stores before pupating. Overwintering, it emerges as an adult the following spring, when the males and females will mate.

As a parasitic species, the Common Mourning Bee has no pollen-collecting features on its body, for the simple reason that it does not need to gather pollen to feed its young. The flower bee host has already done all the hard work and provisioned the nest.

The Common Mourning Bee does, however, feed itself with nectar from a wide variety of spring and early summer flowers. These include dandelions, gorse, wallflowers (*Erysimum spp.* and *Erysimum bicolor*) and vetches.

Wall flower

SOLITARY BEES

'THE BIG 8'

This is a term used to group the most common bumblebees found in the UK:

1. Buff-tailed Bumblebee	*5. Common Carder Bee*
2. Early Bumblebee	*6. Tree Bumblebee*
3. White-tailed Bumblebee	*7. Garden Bumblebee*
4. Red-tailed Bumblebee	*8. Heath Bumblebee*

BUMBLEBEE FARMING

Most people don't know that there is an established international trade in factory-farmed bumblebees. It's publicity shy, making it hard to work out how many nests have been shipped globally, but numbers run into the millions over about 30 years.

Several different species are farmed, but the trade is dominated by two species, with European facilities breeding the Buff-tailed Bumblebee (*Bombus terrestris*) and the US using their native Common Eastern Bumblebee (*Bombus impatiens*).

The bumblebee nests are air freighted around the world to pollinate glasshouse crops, especially tomatoes and peppers. Farmers are told to destroy the nests afterwards, but of course there are always ways out of the greenhouses, allowing imported bees to escape, taking their diseases and parasites with them.

South America, for instance, is awash with Buff-tailed Bumblebees from Europe, with negative outcomes for many native species, including the world's largest bumblebee, the enormous *Bombus dahlbomii*, sometimes called the 'flying mouse', which lives in the Andes. This was a common insect until 20 years ago and the introduction of the Buff-tails. Now it's teetering on the edge of extinction.

FACTS ABOUT BUMBLEBEES

The world has around 250 species of bumblebee, living primarily in northern temperate zones of Europe, Asia and North America. In the southern hemisphere there are native species in South America and Indonesia.

The UK has 24 distinct species of bumblebee (18 true bumblebees and six parasitic 'cuckoo' species), while the USA numbers 49 and mainland Europe has 68.

Some species occur in many different countries, while other species or sub-species can be unique to small areas. Each has its typical sizes, form and colouring as well as its own habitat and forage preferences. These differences allow us to identify them, but there are some core facts that unite all bumblebees.

- All bumblebees belong to a single genus and have a scientific name beginning with *Bombus*, a word derived from the Latin for humming or buzzing.

- In English, the bumblebee was for many centuries more commonly called a 'humblebee' and, in dialect, a 'dumbledor'.

- Bumblebees have rounder bodies than honeybees, with soft, fuzzy fur called pile. This warm coat allows bumblebees to work in cooler temperatures than honeybees, and you will see them foraging earlier and later than many other bees. They rarely forage in extremely hot weather.

- Like honeybees, bumblebees have the ability to shiver their thoracic flight muscles to create body heat. Honeybees use this mechanism to maintain a steady hive temperature in cold months. Bumblebees use it both to incubate their eggs and to buzz pollinate (releasing sticky pollens by creating vibrations).

- The twin talents of buzz pollination and the ability to work in cooler conditions have made bumblebees commercially useful as specialist pollinators. Bumblebee nests are farmed and shipped around the world, with escapes and carelessly discarded nests having cataclysmic results for native bee populations (see pages 12–14).

- Although all are long-tongued (see page 58) compared with other bees, bumblebees themselves are sub-classified into long-, short- or mid-length-tongued species. This has implications for the plants they visit. Longer tongues allow the bee to access a wider range of plants, especially those with deep or trumpet-shaped flowers.

- Only female bumblebees have stings, but unlike honeybees, they can retract and re-use their stinger as it is part of their reproductive system.

- Bumblebees are not aggressive, and females rarely sting unless defending their nests from disturbances. Queens also use their stingers on other queens when competing for nest sites.

- Bumblebees are social bees. They live in relatively short-lived colonies, founded annually when the young, mated queens emerge from solitary winter hibernation. Some bumblebee species build more than one nest per season.

- The so-called 'cuckoo' species (see page 21) of bumblebees do not build nests or gather pollen as they are not raising their own young.

- Bumblebee queens live for one season only, unlike honeybee queens who can live for several years.

- Most bumblebee species nest on or under the ground, especially favouring sites previously occupied by small creatures such as mice, which leave behind nests composed of moss, fine grasses, feathers and other soft materials.

- Once a bumblebee queen has found a site and is ready to lay, she uses wax extruded from special glands and scraped from her body to build cells into which she lays egg clusters that she then incubates, generating heat by shivering her flight muscles. She also builds tiny wax 'larder' pots to store nectar that both feeds adult bees and is mixed with pollen for the brood.

- Bumblebees store pollen in the nest to feed the developing larvae. Long-tongued species are 'pocket makers', storing pollen close to the larvae so that they can feed themselves. Shorter-tongued bumblebees are 'pollen storers', keeping the pollen in separate wax vessels away from the larvae. The workers feed the larvae from there, while the foraging bees keep stores topped up.

- At first, the queen lays only female workers, which grow up to take over the work of the colony, including tending the brood and foraging to meet their needs. The queen will usually not leave the nest again once the workforce is up to strength.

- Later in the season, the queen lays male bees (drones) and new queens (gynes), setting the foundation for new generations. Male bumblebees leave the nest to fend for themselves as soon as they can fly.

- Bumblebee drones often congregate and can use various behaviours to attract or pounce on emerging young queens. You may also find them, singly or in groups, feeding from or fast asleep in flowers that offer them sustenance, shelter and warmth.

- Once they have mated with the waiting drones, young queens often return to their birthplace nest, to fatten themselves up for the winter ahead. Later, they find themselves a safe hibernation site, emerging months later to start their own colonies.

- Sightings of non-hibernating urban bumblebee queens have been attributed to climate change. Cities are also generally warmer than the countryside.

GYPSY CUCKOO BEE

The fabulously named Gypsy Cuckoo Bee fully lives up to its name as one of the parasitic species that cleverly gets other bumblebees to raise its young. There are six cuckoo bumblebee species in the UK and mainland Europe, an additional four in Europe only and 29 in the US and Canada.

Cuckoo bumblebee species do not produce worker bees, because they have no colony of their own that needs looking after. The queens and the males forage only for themselves and cuckoo bees have no pollen baskets on their legs.

queen
♀

APPROXIMATE SIZE:
Queen 15–20 mm (0.59–0.79 in)
Male 11–17 mm (0.43–0.67 in)

SCIENTIFIC NAME:
Bombus bohemicus
FAMILY: *Apidae*

WHERE & WHEN YOU'LL SEE THEM

This is one of Europe's most common cuckoo bees, found from Britain to Turkey and eastern Russia. In Britain, it is more widespread in the north. A North American resident too, it occurs in Canada and the US, in the east, mid-west and Alaska (and is possibly the same species as another North American cuckoo bee, *Bombus ashtoni*.)

Cuckoo bumblebees are often associated with particular host species. In the Gypsy's case this is three white-tailed bumblebees; *Bombus magnus*, *B. cryptarum* and *B. lucorum*.

Mated the previous year, Gypsy Cuckoo queens emerge from hibernation in April/May, later than their host species. This gives potential hosts time to get their nests set up with a strong colony of workers, paving the way for the Gypsy's nest takeover.

HABITAT & LIFE CYCLE

Having fattened herself up foraging while her ovaries develop, the Gypsy Cuckoo queen tracks down target host nests through her species-specific trail pheromones. These enable her not only to find potential nests, but also to identify the strongest and most viable ones.

Identifying a nest, she moves in, mimicking its smell to provide a cloak of invisibility and hopefully fooling the workers into allowing her to stay. Once there, she either kills the host queen or reduces her to worker status. Either way, she also furtively eats or ejects many of the previous queen's eggs, but leaving enough workers to guarantee that her own eggs will be well looked after once she starts laying.

The Gypsy dominates the nest through physical aggression and her pheromone scent, which unites the host workers. Maintaining dominance is essential. If her cover is blown, the workforce will revolt, begin to lay their own eggs, and either kill or fail to look after the cuckoo brood.

If she's successful though, the hosts will raise her brood for her, ensuring the Gypsy Cuckoo queen's genes are passed on via her sons and daughter queens.

SUPPORTING THIS BEE

Although it may seem odd to consider supporting cuckoo species that parasitize other bees' nests, Gypsy Cuckoo Bees play an important role in the ecosystem and it's worth knowing the plants they visit, all of which support many other pollinators.

(Once the Gypsy Cuckoo has established herself within a host colony, she feeds on whatever they bring in.)

Trees and bushes: Bramble/ blackberry, bilberry, cotoneaster, raspberry, sycamore, willow.

Smaller plants: Bistort, bugle, clovers, cornflower, dandelion, heathers, knapweed, lavenders, rosebay willow herb, scabious, thistles, wild thyme.

Cornflowers

GARDEN BUMBLEBEE

Garden bumblebees have the longest tongue of any British bumblebee – up to 2 cm (¾ in) in length and perfectly designed for reaching down into deep flowers such as foxgloves and honeysuckles. Terrific pollinators, they visit masses of flowers on every outing. Sometimes too busy to put their long tongue away between flowers, they'll fly with it stuck out in front of them.

Garden bumblebees have a longer head and slimmer body than many other species. Look for their bright yellow collar and midriff band and their white tail, markings shared by the queen, males and workers (although they can all be darker, making them less easy to identify).

queen

♀

APPROXIMATE SIZE:
Queen 17–20 mm (0.67–0.79 in)
Worker 11–17 mm (0.43–0.67 in)
Male 14–15 mm (0.55–0.59 in)

SCIENTIFIC NAME:
Bombus hortorum
FAMILY: *Apidae*

WHERE & WHEN YOU'LL SEE THEM

Concerns have been raised about whether this species is now in decline, as it inhabits woodland/farmland margins, making it susceptible to pesticide exposure. At the moment at least, Garden Bumblebees remain common in the British Isles, through England, Scotland and Wales and up into Orkney and the Shetland Isles. They are also common right across mainland Europe and into northern and central Asia. The species is also found in Iceland and has been introduced to New Zealand and the USA, especially Florida.

In the northern hemisphere, look for them from March to July. They can sometimes rear a second generation and be seen until late September. Active queens have occasionally been recorded in winter, having failed to hibernate, probably due to climate change. The typical place to see Garden Bumblebees is sunny areas of grassland, along the flowery boundaries of fields and woodland. Public and private gardens suit them well, too. When foraging, they 'trapline', using identical routes to visit the same feeding flower patches for several days at a time.

Garden Bumblebees typically nest under cover, either above ground or up to 50 cm (20 in) underground, but this species has also been known to nest in human-made spaces such as buckets, under sheds or in nest boxes intended for other creatures. If you find a nest, try not to disturb it. They are not aggressive, their colonies are small (up to 100 bees) and they will have dispersed by the end of summer.

Mated queens emerge from their solitary hibernation from March onwards, immediately seeking nectar to give them energy to fly and pollen to develop their ovaries. Foraging on a wide variety of plants and then resting for part of the day, they gradually build up strength, but their priority is to find their own nest site to start a new colony.

Her site claimed, the queen prepares the nest using wax produced from her own body to build cells, into which she lays clusters of eight eggs. She will also shape the wax into tiny pots to hold energy-giving nectar. Garden Bumblebees are 'pocket makers', supplying each cell with its own protein-rich pollen reserves and keeping them topped up until the larvae turn themselves into cocoons.

The first eggs to hatch are worker females, which take over all brood care, wax production and foraging, leaving the queen to lay. Later in the cycle she switches to producing males and future queens.

Once they have emerged from the nest and mated, future queens often return to their colony of origin where they forage to feed themselves up. Later, they find a place to hibernate, emerging the following spring to start their own colonies. In warmer areas they may raise a second generation, and it will be their daughters that overwinter.

SUPPORTING THIS BEE

Finding pollen and nectar early in the year gives the emerging queens the energy to find nest sites and start their colony. The forage plants that sustain the colony include both wild and cultivated flowers. Here are some of the key species:

Trees and bushes: Apple, bramble/blackberry, ceanothus (aka Californian lilac), flowering currant, honeysuckle.

Smaller flowers: Aconite (especially monkshood), aquilegia, bugle, clovers, comfrey, dandelion, deadnettles (including ground ivy and delphiniums, especially larkspur), foxgloves, knapweed, lavender, primrose, thistles, vetches.

SOCIAL BEES

TREE BUMBLEBEE

Spreading from Europe, Tree Bumblebees were first seen in the UK in 2001 but are now common, having become one of 'The Big 8' (see page 94). They have a showy mating behaviour, often leading people to confuse them with swarming honeybees.

The secret of the Tree Bumblebee's success is being a generalist feeder, happy on upland heath and woodlands, but also enjoying a wide range of urban locations, such as gardens, parks, allotments and scruffy, overlooked corners. Unusually for a bumblebee, it's a tree-nesting rather than a ground-nesting species, and is also at home with high-level situations in the built-up environment. This is one of the easiest bumblebees to spot, as the queen, workers and males all have a fluffy ginger/brown thorax, black abdomen and a big white tail.

worker

♀

APPROXIMATE SIZE:
Queen 15–20 mm (0.59–0.79 in)
Worker 11 mm (0.43 in)
Male 13 mm (0.51 in)

SCIENTIFIC NAME: *Bombus hypnorum*
FAMILY: *Apidea*

WHERE & WHEN YOU'LL SEE THEM

Well established across England and Wales and advancing into Scotland and now Ireland, Tree Bumblebees are common in northern Europe and north-eastern Asia too. They have also populated urban areas of Iceland. Evolved to nest in trees on woodland margins, they have happily adapted to other territories, including many human-made spaces, populating bird boxes, loft spaces and holes in walls. Occasionally they nest in or closer to the ground. Tree Bumblebees are typically seen between March and the end of summer. Their queens are one of the first species to emerge from hibernation and can then be seen investigating holes to find the perfect nest site.

HABITAT & LIFE CYCLE

Tree Bumblebees can be 'double brooders', producing two generations in a year. To achieve this, the original queen needs to lay her new queens early enough to give them time to mate, find a nest site and raise a colony of their own before winter. You may see active queens until early winter.

A typical Tree Bumblebee colony numbers around 150 bees (but occasionally up to 300) with a laying queen and female workers tending the young. As a shorter-tongued species, they keep their pollen stores separate from the larvae, constantly replenishing the supply by foraging outside the nest on flowers. Nectar reserves stored in small wax pots are also kept topped up to feed adults. Although not aggressive, Tree Bumblebees stoutly defend their nest if they feel threatened.

They also have a distinctive mating behaviour that involves clouds of bees congregating outside nest entrances during the day, which is often misinterpreted as swarming. This happens especially in May and June and sometimes continues for hours at a time. There's nothing to worry about, though, as this is a wonderful piece of bee theatre called nest surveillance or 'lekking'. That dancing cloud of bees is a group of hopeful males, patrolling and lying in wait to pounce on young, unmated queens emerging from the nest. Occasional mid-air collisions occur when one overexcited male mistakes another for a queen.

Once the young queens do finally emerge, the males jostle and barge to pair up with them. This can look as if they are fighting, as the queens put up some resistance and can sometimes sting males to death. Bees are frequently knocked out of the air in the process. But once paired they stay coupled for some time and even fly off together, though they usually remain on the ground. The mated queen then returns to the nest where she was born and feeds herself up, possibly ahead of starting a late new colony or, more usually, finding a safe place to hibernate for the winter.

SUPPORTING THIS BEE

Tree Bumblebees appreciate a wide range of plants on which to forage. Early pollen sources such as pussy willow are always valuable to emerging queens. Other plants they enjoy include:

Trees and bushes: Apple, blackberry, blackcurrants, ceanothus (Californian lilac), cherry, cotoneaster, fuchsia, gooseberry, limes (linden), pussy willow, raspberry, rhododendron, wild forms of roses (e.g. *Rosa canina*, *R. rugosa* and *R. tomentosa*), snowberry.

Smaller flowers: Aconite (especially monkshood), autumn/winter heathers, chives, comfrey, delphinium (especially larkspur), foxgloves, grape hyacinth, red clover.

Habitat: Bird boxes and special bumblebee nesting boxes may provide nesting spaces. Unlike many bumblebee species, Tree Bumblebees can be defensive of their territory, so are best sited away such as sheds.

SOCIAL BEES

HEATH BUMBLEBEE

The geographical distribution of the Heath Bumblebee is remarkable, extending from Britain across mainland Europe and into northern Asia as far as the Bering Sea on the Northern Pacific coast. It is also found in Canada and Alaska, as well as beyond the Arctic Circle in Russia and Scandinavia.

People use words such as, shaggy, and, scruffy, to describe the endearingly unkempt appearance of this fairly small, but distinctly furry bee. Its coat (or pile) is a good way to tell it apart from the better groomed and generally larger Garden Bumblebee (see page 100) with which it is often confused, especially as they both have white tails.

queen

♀

APPROXIMATE SIZE:
Queen 13–15 mm (0.51–0.59 in)
Worker 10–12 mm (0.39–0.47 in)
Male 11–14 mm (0.43–0.55 in)

SCIENTIFIC NAME: *Bombus jonellus*
FAMILY: *Apidea*

WHERE & WHEN YOU'LL SEE THEM

A Heath Bumblebee safari would take you to an astonishing range of environments, from Britain's ling heather moors to the grassy coastal machair of the Hebrides, and from the Pyrenees to the deep forests of Poland. In Russia you would find this bee within the unique ecosystems of both the taiga snow forest in Siberia and the tundra, one of the harshest environments on earth, where summer lasts only 6–10 weeks. It is also found in the challenging climates of northern US and Canada.

In warmer, southerly areas, queens emerge from hibernation in March to spend time strengthening themselves and searching for the ideal nest site. Her worker daughters and males are on the wing in April and daughter queens in May. This timing often allows a second generation to be raised in a single season in some areas. Significantly cooler northern environments see queens emerging later, leaving time for only one generation during the summer.

HABITAT & LIFE CYCLE

True to its name, the Heath Bumblebee is at its most abundant on heathland and moors, but is equally at home on coastal marshes and dunes, chalk grasslands and other flower-rich environments. In urban areas, gardens and parks suit it well. But as we've seen from its range, its ability to adapt long term to different global environments is impressive.

Heath Bumblebee queens generally seek out either underground nesting sites or surface areas where they can bury the nest in dense vegetation. Sometimes they also choose aerial sites such as bird boxes, deserted squirrel dreys or roof voids. Like many bumblebee species, they have been reported nesting in some fairly eccentric sites, including rolled-up carpets and cushions left in a shed.

Short tongued, Heath Bumblebees forage across a wide range of flora, collecting nectar and pollen. Within the nest, the nectar feeds adult bees, while the pollen is stored in the wax pots from which the workers then feed the brood.

Heath bumblebees have a short colony cycle, which makes it easier for them to raise a second generation in the same year. Their nests tend to be small, sometimes numbering as few as 50 workers. Once males have left the colony to fend for themselves they run high-level patrols, setting out their wares by scent-marking leaves and twigs to attract the unmated queens when they emerge from the nest. Once mated, the new queens continue to forage, in preparation for their solitary winter hibernation. (The males, as usual for bees, die once their only job – mating – is accomplished.)

SUPPORTING THIS BEE

Heath Bumblebees feed mostly on heathland plants suited to their short tongues.

Trees and bushes: Bramble/ blackberry, lingonberry, rhododendron, willow.

Smaller flowers: Bell and ling heathers (*Erica spp.* and *Calluna*), bird's-foot trefoil, clovers, dandelion, deadnettles, eyebright, hawkbits, knapweed, melilot, purple loosestrife, scabious, teasels, thistles, thyme, viper's bugloss.

Habitat: Given its wide variety of nesting habits, this is one of the bumblebee species that might just be attracted to a nesting box (see page 130). It also likes quiet, out-of-the-way places, so a little healthy neglect in some corners of your garden may provide just the place, and will not go unnoticed by other wildlife either.

SOCIAL BEES

RED-TAILED BUMBLEBEE

Nature is relentless in its pragmatism. Red-tailed Bumblebee workers sometimes eat their own queen's eggs, no matter how hard she fights back by physically head-butting her daughters. And the queen may already have eaten some of the workers' eggs, laid when their ovaries activated in response to her failing dominance over the nest.

Red-tailed queens are significantly larger than the males and workers, but they share the same velvety black bodies and bright red tails, which makes them easy to spot. Males also sport a bright yellow collar, sometimes with a natty matching moustache.

♂ *male*

APPROXIMATE SIZE:
Queen 20–22 mm (0.66–0.86 in)
Worker 11–16 mm (0.43–0.63 in)
Male 14–16 mm (0.55–0.63 in)

SCIENTIFIC NAME:
Bombus lapidarius
FAMILY: *Apidae*

WHERE & WHEN YOU'LL SEE THEM

Widespread through Britain and Ireland, these bumblebees are now extending their range in Scotland. They are widespread too in central Europe, and found as far south as Greece and as far north as Finland.

The name *lapidarius* is associated with stones and gemstones and is said to reference this species' glowingly bright red tail. This is a large bumblebee and you can spot queens out foraging in early spring, sometimes even

as early as March. By early April they will be seen flying at low level, painstakingly investigating potential, usually underground, nest sites. From June onwards you may see both young males and females. In July and August you can also find males patrolling mating circuits (see opposite).

HABITAT & LIFE CYCLE

Red-tails are creatures of grassland, scrub, brownfield sites and fairly open woodland. But they have also adapted to urban living, so nest sites can vary from holes vacated by previous mammal tenants to short grass, bare earth, small hollows in the ground, bird boxes and spaces in or close to bricks or concrete, where they probably enjoy retained warmth.

Colony sizes vary but larger ones can number up to 300 workers at the peak of the season in July/August. As the colony breaks down at the end of the summer, the queen's pheromones, which usually suppress the worker's ovaries, can falter. Her unfertilized worker daughters will then try to eat her eggs and lay their own instead, but they cannot build a viable colony as (being unmated) they can only lay males. Worker revolts are not unique to Red-tailed Bumblebees, but they are one of the key species in which this behaviour has been seen. Also not unique, but still remarkable, is the Red-tailed males' patrolling behaviour. While waiting for the young queens to emerge, males patrol regular pathways, stopping at various tall points to replenish scent marks on the mating circuit they've established. Up to 20 bees at a time can join a patrol but young queens seem underwhelmed by their efforts and mating happens with the usual free-for-all scramble.

Newly mated queens hibernate in loose soil. Emerging the following spring, they are said to find dandelions and bluebells especially attractive among the array of early forage on offer, which they access to build

themselves up for nest hunting, nest building and brood rearing.

SUPPORTING THIS BEE

Supplying queens with pollen as they emerge from their winter hibernation helps nourish them as they gather strength. The colonies they build then need nectar and pollen from a good range of wild and cultivated forage to take them through into early autumn. Like so many other pollinators, these comparatively short-tongued bumblebees enjoy herb garden plantings, including chives, thyme, sage, lavender, borage and marjoram. They are also known to pollinate field beans and oilseed rape crops. Here is a list of some of their other preferred forage:

Trees and bushes: Apple, berberis, cherry, blackthorn, bramble/ blackberry, broom, ceanothus/ Californian lilac, flowering currant, hebe, laburnum, mahonia, mallow, willow.

Smaller flowers: Asters, bell heathers, bird's-foot trefoil, bluebell, burdock, busy lizzie, buttercups, clover, comfrey (*Symphytum officinale* and others), common/field poppy, crocus, dandelion, deadnettle, knapweed, scabious, sedum (stonecrop), simple-flowered dahlias, St. John's wort, teasels, thistles, tree lupin, vetches, viper's bugloss, wallflowers.

SOCIAL BEES

COMMON CARDER BEE

*Carder bumblebees get their name because they use bristles on their legs to comb
(or 'card') together soft materials, such as moss and dried grass, to create, with the
addition of wax, a well-defined and insulated nest. This construction creates a cosy
shelter for the brood and helps to maintain the correct nest temperature.*

*This pretty ginger-furred bumblebee is an early-emerging species and also
one of the latest you'll see in the year, with its young queens gathering
pre-hibernation food as late as November.*

worker

♀

APPROXIMATE SIZE:
Queen 13–17 mm (0.51–0.67 in)
Worker 8–13 mm (0.31–0.51 in)
Male 11 mm (0.43 in)

SCIENTIFIC NAME:
Bombus pascuorum
FAMILY: *Apidea*

WHERE & WHEN YOU'LL SEE THEM

Widespread across Britain and
into Ireland, and just as frequently
occurring in mainland Europe, this
is one of the most commonly seen
garden bumblebees. The mated queens
emerge from hibernation in April
or May and can be spotted checking
out nest sites and feeding widely.
This fairly long-tongued species is a
generalist feeder, so look for Common
Carders anywhere there are flowers,
especially because they populate such
a wide range of different habitats, rural
and urban, from domestic gardens to
meadow and pastureland, woodlands
and heaths. Although it is not clear
whether they can raise a second brood
in a season, the fact that the foragers
are seen as late as October/November
suggests that this is happening.

HABITAT & LIFE CYCLE

The Common Carder prefers to nest
at or just below ground level, choosing
spots under hedges or in leaf litter,
mossy patches or tufty patches of
unmown grass. This can put them
at risk from lawn mowers or, in the
country, agricultural machinery.

This is an adaptable bee, though, and some queens settle on using disused mouse holes close to the surface, or setting their sights even higher, taking over abandoned birds' nests. Outbuildings such as sheds and barns may also contain cavities that appeal.

Once she has identified a good nest site, the queen uses dry grass, moss and other soft materials to weave her small, hollow nest. Inside this, she builds her wax nest cups, laying five to 15 eggs into each. Once the nest is populated, the worker bees take over the hard work of foraging and brood care, while the queen focuses on laying. The queen and later, her workers, use wax from her body to form tiny reservoir pots around 20 mm (0.79 in) high, which are filled with nectar to feed adult bees. Common Carder nests are not especially large, containing between 50 and 150 individuals at their peak in August. Around this time, the male bumblebees leave the nest and build themselves up, ready to pounce on the young queens emerging a little later. Once mated, the new queens either start a second generation in that season or prepare themselves for hibernation, ready to emerge the following spring and begin the cycle once more.

SUPPORTING THIS BEE

The spring-emerging queens, urgently in need of pollen, are a major pollinator of fruit trees. Common Carders have an extremely long tongues, which allows them to access some deep and complicated flower structures. While they forage nectar from a wide range of wild and cultivated plants (far, far too wide to list comprehensively here), they seem to have a more limited shopping list for their pollen stores, mainly members of the *Fabaceae* (pea/bean) family.

They are also major visitors to herb gardens, as they love lavenders, mints, thymes, catmints, verbenas, rosemary bushes and other members of the *Lamiaceae* (mint/sage/deadnettle) family, which are important resources for so many different bees and pollinator garden staples.

Trees and bushes: Apple and many other fruiting trees, including blackthorn, bramble/blackberry, cherries, flowering currants, raspberry. Also berberis (or barberry), gorse, hibiscus, horse chestnut, jasmine, lilac, mahonia, rhododendron, snowberry, wiegela.

Smaller flowers: Bugle, bird's-foot trefoil, comfrey (*Symphytum officinale* and others), dandelion, red and white deadnettles, clovers, foxglove, hardy geraniums/cranesbills, heather, knapweed, michaelmas daisy, scabious, sedum (Stonecrop), thistles, vetches, viper's bugloss.

Habitat: Planting is the most important way to support these bees.

EARLY BUMBLEBEE

This smallish bumblebee is one of the first to emerge in spring. It is also one of the species in which queens have been known to control the nest through physical behaviour rather than pheromones, managing daughter workers through biting and aggressive head-butting.

Early Bumblebees, especially males, have long, bristly coats, making their bodies seem particularly round and fluffy. A short-tongued species, they feed from a wide variety of flowers, from early through to late-season forage.

♂ *male*

APPROXIMATE SIZE
Queen 13 mm (0.51 in)
Worker 10 mm (0.39 in)
Male 10 mm (0.39 in)

SCIENTIFIC NAME:
Bombus pratorum
FAMILY: *Apidae*

WHERE & WHEN YOU'LL SEE THEM

Early Bumblebees are at home in a huge range of urban and rural environments, from scrub and woodland to roadsides, coastal marshes, gardens and brownfield sites. Neglected or re-wilded areas with plenty of wild bramble suit them perfectly.

Found across Britain, Ireland and much of mainland Europe, from the Mediterranean to the Arctic, this bee is also seen in Turkey and Iran. Queens can be spotted as early as February in warmer climates, later in cooler regions. An early start gives the potential to occasionally have two, or even three, nest cycles in the year, so in warmer areas you may see foraging bees as late as October.

HABITAT & LIFE CYCLE

Early Bumblebees are incredibly adaptable and resourceful, nesting above or below ground, in rodent burrows, bird boxes, roof spaces, bushes and even less obvious locations, such as amongst shed clutter.

Their nests are relatively small, typically around 100 bees. Being short-tongued, they are a pollen-storing species, keeping food in tiny wax pots from which the workers feed the brood.

This species is the main host for the parasitic Forest Cuckoo Bumblebee queens (*Bombus sylvestris*) who tricks Early Bumblebee workers into feeding and rearing her young for her (see the technique used by the Gypsy Cuckoo bee on page 98).

Early Bumblebees are also known for robbing nectar from flowers such as comfrey, which are too deep for a short tongue. Simply biting a hole in the base of the flower gives them quick access to the sugar-rich nectar reward. Honeybees, also short tongued, will then often use the same holes. All of this happens without the bees directly pollinating the plant, the tremors created by their visits may loosen the pollen enough for some fertilization to take place.

SUPPORTING THIS BEE

Because it emerges so early, the success of this species depends on having plenty of early forage. Willow catkins are vital to this and many other bee species that need to access winter-into-spring pollen. Mahonia is another excellent source of early pollen, as are japonicas and hellebores. Below is a list of plants that please both Early Bumblebees and many other pollinators.

Trees and bushes: Bramble/blackberry, blackthorn, cherry, cotoneaster, flowering currant, hebe, hellebores, japonica, raspberry, rhododendron, mahonia, viburnum, willow.

Smaller flowers: Asters, bell heathers, clovers, comfrey, deadnettles, devil's bit scabious, ground ivy, hardy geraniums/cranesbills, lungwort, vetches.

Habitat: Wild, brambly areas in the garden are a good bet for attracting this species, offering a safe space with a major forage source to hand.

Goat Willow Catkins

SOCIAL BEES

BUFF-TAILED BUMBLEBEE

As well as living in the wild, Buff-tails are bred commercially, and their nests exported to aid glasshouse pollination of crops, especially tomatoes. Escapees have become invasive species in places such as Chile, Argentina, Japan and Tasmania, often compromising native bees. Not endangered, they are sometimes used in research, including investigations into bumblebees' capacity for learning, which turns out to be impressive (see pages 31–32).

Strangely, only the queen has a buff tail. She's also very large and not hard to spot. Her workers and males have paler tails that make it hard to differentiate them from White-tailed species. The trick is to look for a slim buff stripe just where their white tail meets the black stripe above.

queen

♀

APPROXIMATE SIZE:
Queen 18–20 mm (0.71–0.79 in)
Worker 11–16 mm (0.42–0.63 in)
Male 14–16 mm (0.55–0.63 in)

SCIENTIFIC NAME:
Bombus terrestris
FAMILY: *Apidea*

WHERE & WHEN YOU'LL SEE THEM

This is an adaptable bumblebee species, at home in urban and rural environments. Widespread in the south of England, they extend into Wales, through the Midlands and up into the north of Scotland. Ireland has good populations too. Aside from the numerous countries where they have been commercially imported as pollinators, they have a native range that includes central and southern Europe, running east into Afghanistan. Their northerly range goes as far as Helsinki and Siberia's Altai Mountains.

Queens emerge late in February and her first workers will be foraging in April. The first males and new queens can be seen in late May. This species is not only able to raise a second generation in the same year, but sometimes even a third, so you may see them foraging as late as October or even on warm winter days.

Mated queens seeking nest sites fly close the ground, often near to hedges or grassy margins. Other places to spot prospecting queens include around the bottom of sheds, on the banks of waterways, in open woodland and even among ivy. Rough grassland is also popular but they are extremely flexible in their site selection.

HABITAT & LIFE CYCLE

Buff-tails create large colonies in nests that are often accessed via downward sloping tunnels up to 2 m (6½ ft) long, with a canopy built from wax and pollen. Guard bees patrol the tunnel to raise the alarm and send a cloud of workers flying outside the nest to repel would-be intruders or predators if needed.

They have short tongues and store pollen for the brood in wax pots. As with all bumblebees, the wax used in building the nest originates first from the body of the queen and later from her daughter workers. The wax is made into vessels holding nectar and pollen and is also continuously used to build and enlarge the cells as the larvae grow. Once these have hatched, it is recycled into new cells and vessels.

Buff-tails are well known for robbing nectar from deep flowers such as honeysuckle and field beans, which their tongues are too short to access

in the traditional way. To get to the sweetness within, they simply bite into the flower to make an access hole, which can then also be used by other bumblebees and honeybees. Although this bypasses the classic pollen transfer via the bee's body, researchers believe that their shaking of the flower as they drink often achieves pollination anyway.

Mated queens hibernate alone in a variety of underground places or may even raise an overwinter generation.

SUPPORTING THIS BEE

With a relatively short tongue, Buff-tails need accessible flowers. Early- and late-flowering shrubs are vital to them, as is a good variety of spring, summer and autumn cultivated plants. Equally important are wildflowers, many of them with fabulous names that just roll off the tongue – hoary plantain, black horehound, bristly ox-tongue, restharrow, marsh woundwort, purple toadflax. Many other bees love these too.

In the kitchen garden, Buff-tails enjoy borage, chives, rosemary, marjoram, lavender and sage. They are also pollinators of crops such as oilseed rape and greenhouse tomatoes.

SOCIAL BEES

Here are some other plants helpful to these very adaptable feeders:

Trees and bushes: Bramble/ blackberry, blackthorn, broom, buddleja, ceanothus (or Californian lilac), cherry, dogwood, flowering currant, flowering ivy, gorse, hebe, mahonia, mallow, prive, rhododendron, snowberry, tree germander (*Teucrium*, willow, winter/ sweet box), winter honeysuckle.

Smaller flowers: Begonia, bird's-foot trefoil, bugle, burdock, clovers, crocus, comfrey (*Symphytum officinale* and others), daffodils, dandelion, deadnettles, echinacea, hardy geraniums/cranesbills, heather (*Erica spp.* and Calluna), knapweed, michaelmas daisy, phacelia, scabious, sedum (Stonecrop), thistles, tree lupin, vetches, viper's bugloss.

Habitat: The most helpful thing you can do for these bees is to plant suitable forage and leave some marginal areas of the garden uncultivated, with bare earth or rough grass. Sunny banks and areas close to nettle beds or hedges are popular places for queens to search out their ideal home. Equally, they may just find a place in a barn or shed. See page 24 for what to do if you find a bumblebee nest.

Common Teasel

HONEYBEE SPECIES

There are often said to be seven honeybee species (although up to 11 have been suggested) of which only the Western Honeybee (on the following pages) has significant global distribution. Six other honeybee species are listed below. All valuable pollinators, their social organization and life cycle are broadly the same, but differ substantially in the detail.

Apis cerana, **THE EASTERN HONEYBEE,** found in south and south-east Asia. It can be seen both wild and domesticated.

Apis dorsata, **THE GIANT HONEYBEE,** lives wild in the forests of south and south-east Asia. It has a famous subspecies, *Apis laboriosa,* the Giant Himalayan Bee.

Apis florea, **THE DWARF RED HONEYBEE,** occasionally domesticated by humans, but mostly lives wild in south and south-east Asia, as well as some African countries.

Apis andreniformis, **THE DWARF BLACK HONEYBEE,** sometimes kept, but mostly lives wild in tropical and subtropical south-east Asia

Apis koschevnikovi, **THE RED BEE OF SABAH,** lives wild in Borneo's tropical forests.

Apis nigrocincta, **THE BLACK-BANDED WILD HONEYBEE,** found in the Philippines and Indonesia.

The 500+ species of stingless bee, or Meliponines, are not categorized as true honeybees, although they are closely related. Sometimes domesticated, they mainly live wild in tropical and sub-tropical regions including Australia, Africa, south-east Asia and Central and South America.

WILD HONEYBEE

The majority of the world's numerous honeybees are the Western, or European, Honeybee (Apis mellifera), kept in human-maintained apiaries. But they, sub-species and other more localized honeybee species are still found wild in many countries, especially where there is extensive native forest.

This is because honeybees' primary affiliation remains with the trees with which they co-evolved over millions of years. Trees provide both a significant proportion of honeybees' preferred forage and ideal nest sites, out of reach of traditional predators such as bears. Some honeybees living wild are feral colonies that have absconded from human management. Others come from far older lines that have always lived wild.

♂ *worker*

APPROXIMATE SIZE:
Queen 18–20 mm (0.71–0.79 in)
Worker 10–15 mm (0.39–0.59 in)
Male (Drone) 15–17 mm
(0.59–0.67 in)

SCIENTIFIC NAME: *Apis mellifera*
(Western, or European, Honeybee)
FAMILY: *Apidae*

WHERE & WHEN YOU'LL SEE THEM

Despite its name, recent genome sequencing suggests that the Western Honeybee originated in Asia, from where it spread widely over time. It is the most adaptable of all bee species in its feeding preferences, making it an efficient pollinator in a wide range of environments. In consequence, it has now been transported all over the planet by humans and is our most widespread honeybee species, found on every continent except Antarctica.

It has more than 40 specialized subspecies, which have adapted to thrive in different climates and forage environments. For instance, *Apis mellifera sahariensis*, the Saharan Honeybee, has evolved to forage much further afield than other bees in order to survive in its largely barren environment.

In the wild, most honeybee species like to nest high up within trees but denied these ideal sites, the Western Honeybee can get creative, establishing feral colonies in chimneys, roof and wall cavities and other human-made voids.

At the heart of every colony is a queen with the potential to live for several years. Also in the nest are her shorter-lived daughters (the worker bees) and sons (the drones.) A few young queens may be present as well, housed in special cells and fed a diet rich in the Royal Jelly which nurse bees produce from a gland in their head. Although comprising thousands of individuals, a honeybee colony is, in effect, a single entity, united by the reigning queen's unique pheromone secretions.

A queen honeybee embarks on a single mating flight, mating with numerous drones before returning to the nest with a lifetime's supply of sperm. The drones die after mating. Once mated, she lays thousands of eggs daily at the height of the season. In the northern hemisphere, the laying rate begins to drop after the summer solstice (usually 21 or 22 June) as the now-shrinking colony readies itself for winter's deprivations.

Within the tightly ordered honeybee society, every worker is a female, performing a series of pre-ordained jobs in the weeks between being born and the final stage of her life, when she'll be flying out as a forager – there are many specialist worker roles within the colony, including queen's attendants (who groom and feed her, direct her laying and remove her waste), nurse bees that care for brood, water collectors, mortuary bees that remove the dead and guard bees that patrol the front of the nest.

The wax used to build the comb (within which the queen lays her eggs and where honey and pollen are stored) is extruded from the bodies of young workers and processed and shaped into hexagonal cells by their older sisters. Drones (male bees) do no work in the colony itself; most of those that fail to mate are eventually culled by their sisters.

Scouts fly out from the nest to find the best forage sources, returning to communicate with their sisters, using the wax comb as a dance floor and vibration transmitter as they 'dance' directions and distances (the famous waggle dance, also used for other inter-bee communications). Foraging bees follow those directions to gather nectar, pollen and plant resins. Water too is brought back to the nest when needed, but never stored.

The foraged plant resins are transformed by the bees into propolis, a near-magical substance that they use to medicate themselves and reinforce their nest. Nectar brought back to the nest is concentrated down into honey, much of which is stored in the comb, to feed the colony through days, weeks or even months when forage is unavailable, or bad weather prevents them flying. Foraged pollen is mixed with the bees' gut enzymes and a little nectar, creating a fermented 'bee bread'. That too is stored in the comb's chambers, ready for workers to feed to the larvae.

Honeybees do not hibernate but will generally not fly if the temperature is lower than 10°C (50°F). Clustered around their queen and fuelled by their honey larder, they maintain a constant core temperature within the cluster of at least 27°C (81°F), 'shivering' their thoracic muscles to generate heat.

SUPPORTING THIS BEE

Although relatively short tongued, most honeybee species are adaptable generalists, particularly the Western Honeybee. Ideally, they forage mostly among flowering trees, shrubs and herbaceous perennials, but can draw on pretty much anything accessible to them. So, whereas many other wild bee species are affiliated with just a few flower types, honeybees can forage on those, plus countless other potential nectar and pollen sources. (A recent London honey sample, taken from our hives at Lambeth Palace, showed 83 different pollens.)

This resourcefulness and adaptability is a signature of honeybees generally, but where floral resources are limited or failing, it can place them in direct competition with more specialized wild bees. The competition for floral resources is not disputed, but its true extent remains the subject of often fractious debate between beekeepers and conservationists, with scientists weighing in on both sides. Hives' foraging preferences can also alter the environment, artificially boosting certain plant species through concentrated pollination, and these changes may not suit wild bees or other native wildlife.

To help feed honeybees, wild or hived, focus on planting flowering trees and bushes wherever space allows, and/ or sizeable clumps of herbaceous perennials. These will always be the primary resources that honeybees choose for both their nutrition and their style of floral fidelity feeding, visiting just one type of plant in any foraging trip.

Planting the smaller floral sources in same species clumps mimics the blossom density found in flowering trees and bushes, saving bees valuable energy. Plant for sequential flowering to provide nectars and pollens for as much of the year as possible. This also serves numerous other bee species seeking early and late forage.

Provide a water source. Honeybees need a lot of it and prefer dirty water, so it won't need elaborate maintenance (see page 157).

Bramble

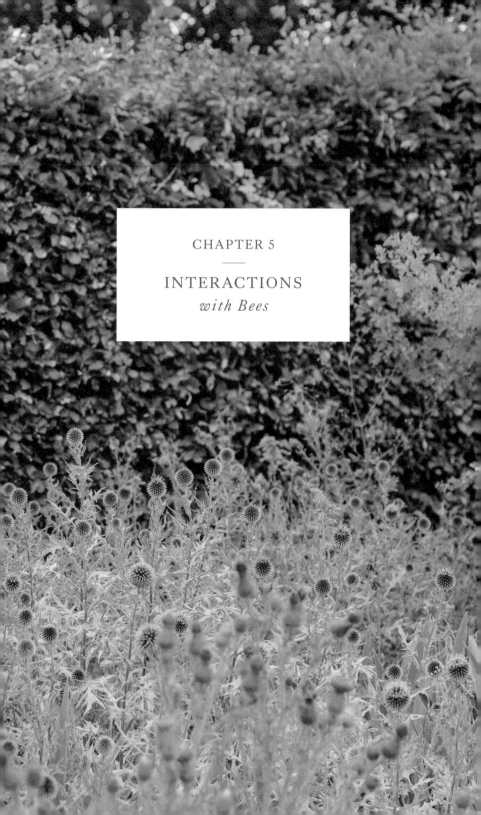

CHAPTER 5

—

INTERACTIONS
with Bees

INTERACTIONS WITH BEES

When we lived in London, our Honey HQ had a front door to the street and people often stopped by to ask advice. One morning, I found an anxious small boy and his mother on the doorstep. Clasped in his hand was, his mother said, a tired bee that he'd scooped up outside. She hadn't actually seen it, but they were wondering whether, perhaps, it could be revived?

I was about to launch into a 'It's very sad, but bees do get worn out and die' life lesson, but he was so hopeful that I just asked him to show me. He opened his palm to reveal... a dead housefly. I took it carefully, decided to say nothing about it not being a bee, gave him a little pot of honey as a thank you, and assured him that I would do my best. Sometimes, it's just better that way.

SPONTANEOUS ENCOUNTERS

HOW TO REVIVE A BEE

Finding a bee on the ground is not an automatic signal to intervene. If it's dead, it's dead, but if it's visibly alive, leave it for a while as it may simply be resting. Researchers have found that perfectly healthy bees, especially bumblebee queens, often rest quietly on the ground for up to 45 minutes at a time. But if the bee is in a risky place, it's worth gently transferring it into a nearby flower. If you are still worried about a bee after some time has passed, here's what to do:

Please never, ever, give a tired bee honey, because it may contain pathogens fatal to bees (but in no way harmful to humans) that, once recovered, it could then spread.

Instead, make up a simple sugar syrup with two parts white sugar dissolved in one part water. Put this onto a teaspoon or into a small flat receptacle and place the bee close to, but not into, the solution. Don't try to force or even encourage the bee to drink. It may take a while, but if rescuable, the bee will extend its tongue to the syrup and drink. Give this process time. With any luck you'll see the bee first refuelling and then starting to perk up, visibly gathering strength. Allow it to rest for a while and hopefully it will fly off or at least be in a stronger state to be placed safely into a flower.

I also recommend the neat 'Beevive' containers of sugar syrup. Small enough to be hung on a keyring, they are a quick, easy way to help a tired bee and are refillable at home[1].

WHAT TO DO IF YOU SEE A SWARM

Only honeybees swarm. It's an entirely natural reproductive process and no threat whatsoever, but can be utterly terrifying on first encounter. Like something you'd see in a horror movie, the sky suddenly blackens with flying bees and their buzzing is indescribably loud. Then – just as abruptly – the noise stops and the bees seem to vanish. The swarm, with a queen at its heart, has temporarily settled in a great mass, usually in a bush or tree, but sometimes in the most unlikely place such as on a car or a shop window. Scout bees fly out to investigate potential new homes, into one of which the swarm will then move.

Don't panic, please don't call emergency services and don't fear that the bees will spontaneously attack anyone. In fact you are never less likely to get stung. The bees are stuffed with honey they've taken on board to help build their new nest and they have only one ambition – to establish a safe new location for their queen and her breakaway colony.

Enjoy watching them, but leave them alone unless they have settled in a completely inappropriate location. If so, call a local beekeeper for advice (not a pest control company). In the UK, you can find swarm collectors through the BBKA website[2].

Some other bee species may appear to be swarming but in reality they are simply congregating. They could be a cloud of eager male bumblebees staking out a nest, waiting for the girls to come out, or the inhabitants of a densely populated solitary bee nesting area. Either way, observe quietly but leave well alone.

[1] BEEVIVE.COM

[2] BBKA.ORG.UK/FIND-A-LOCAL-SWARM-COLLECTOR

WHAT TO DO IF YOU FIND A BEE'S NEST

Again, first principle is to observe quietly and don't interfere in any way. Especially don't ever shake, poke or otherwise disturb any bees.

The only reason to concern yourself about a nest is if it is in an unsafe place or causing problems for humans or other animals. There will usually be ways to leave a nest undisturbed until its natural cycle is finished. I've had a rather pushy nest of White-tailed Bumblebees in my garden shed all summer but we've worked around each other somehow and although I've known exactly where the nest entrance is since early days, it's been fun observing their attempts at distraction.

Wild honeybees generally live high up in trees, but if you have a honeybee nest in a difficult place, make no attempt to move it without advice and help from a beekeeper (see BBKA website). They do show up in some weird places – we once had to remove a perfectly contented colony from under a manhole cover, a bizarre place for them to have taken up residence.

Bumblebee nests can be carefully moved if absolutely necessary, although the colony is unlikely to survive. The Bumblebee Conservation trust website[3] tells you all you need to know about nests.

CAN YOU BUY A BEE A HOME?

Let's talk about 'bee-washing'. This is a term coined by researchers at Toronto's York University and defined as *'a new type of greenwashing where companies mislead consumers to buy products or subscribe to services under the pretence of helping bees. Bee-washing is also used to improve the public image of companies and has become an increasingly common marketing spin'*.

This section looks at artificial habitats and assesses whether they really help wild bees or are just an opportunity for greenwash, and bee-wash, marketing. I've long put off writing this section, because it

[3] BUMBLEBEECONSERVATION.ORG/BEE-FAQS/BUMBLEBEE-NESTS-FREQUENTLY-ASKED-QUESTIONS

touches on my barely suppressed fury about so many 'eco' products and the empty promises they make. If you're reading this book, it's likely to be because you care and genuinely want to know ways to help. But being eager to take new ideas on board can make us ripe targets for marketing and not always equipped to spot the snake-oil offerings.

Greenwash marketing cleverly and cynically exploits people's fears about the future of wildlife and the environment, jumping in with sweet little feel good fixes. The trouble is that, unlike retail, nature doesn't deal in quick fixes. Meaningful progress in changing our environment and supporting our pollinators isn't a package that can be bought online or in a garden centre, no matter how cute it makes the garden look.

What breaks my heart about this eco-bandwagon is how it misdirects people's kindest instincts, betraying the investment of hope they make when buying that designer bee hotel, novelty flower bomb or adorable packet of no-provenance wildflower seeds for their children to scatter. Pointless, often wildly expensive and 100 per cent avoidable.

But there are things out there that really do make a difference. You'll need to roll up your sleeves, though, as there's work ahead...

SOLITARY BEE HOTELS

Bee house or house of horrors? The popular idea is that a bee house/ hotel/condo is a one-size-fits-all commodity helpful to masses of different bees, no matter how crudely inappropriate its design or construction. You can grab one anywhere, even your local petrol station forecourt. All you need to do is buy it, stick it up and walk away. Hooray! You've become a conservationist.

Imagine, though, that you've booked into a hotel. When you get there, you can barely squeeze into the room, everything's filthy and the sheets haven't been changed since the day it was built. There are monsters loose in the corridors, too. This is no place to settle down and start a family.

The point is this: however good your intentions, if you interfere with nature by inviting solitary bees to live in human-made habitats, you are making yourself responsible for those bees. If you want to take on that responsibility, you need to build or buy units that are fit for purpose, and manage them with regular cleaning and renewal.

If you don't, you're putting already-vulnerable bee species at even more risk – of physical damage to their delicate bodies and wings, of exposure to diseases and fungi, and of making them live alongside bee parasites and predators (including mites, wasps, flies and spiders) that love a grubby bee hotel. As Rhiannon Dowling, a biology student at Imperial College London, once expressed it, '*Without proper care, bee hotels become a festering mess*'.

It's a question of personal choice. My personal choice is to provide wild bees with excellent forage and naturally occurring nest sites and then leave nature to its own devices. Other people choose more hands-on approaches, for pleasure or study, and that's all brilliant, as long as you're a conscientious manager for your apian guests. You are making yourself a guardian of their welfare, and offering a shoddy or neglected bee hotel is worse than doing nothing at all.

What's wrong with most bee hotels?

Although marketed as a universal solution, the reality is that bee hotels are only appropriate for a tiny minority of solitary species, principally Mason, Leafcutter and Yellow-faced Bees (see pages 62, 82 and 88). Bear in mind, too, that these bees are solitary – so not characteristically inclined to live in dense 'hive' setups – and they're not checking in for a short rest. They will be occupying the space you're offering for many months, and through whatever the winter holds. You may need to intervene to keep them alive.

Common problems with 'quick-buck' bee hotels:

• No meaningful protection from damp or wet weather.
• The tubes are useless; made from splintery wood or pith-filled bamboo, or non-breathable materials (glass, plastic, metal), all of which lead to condensation and fungal growths.
• The diameters and/or lengths of drilled holes or tubes are the wrong size for the bees they're meant to house.
• The tubes are not sealed at the back and/or are shorter than the box, allowing access for predatory species.

- The wrong length of tube also affects the bees' male/ female egg-laying ratio and could negatively impact conservation.
- Lack of siting instructions – bee hotels must be close to forage resources, and securely fixed in a sunny spot facing south or south-east.
- Lack of guidance on how to protect overwintering nests and how to clean and maintain the unit from season to season.

Solitary bee habitats are specialist kit and for the bees' sake should be as knowledgeably constructed as possible. Look up a couple of makers from my Resources list (see pages 188–193). Their quality guidelines are illuminating, and will also help you if you decide not to buy from them and instead build your own, which is perfectly feasible.

Antidotes to bee-washing

You may enjoy the witty insights and useful guide to good and bad bee houses on the website of American nature blogger and evolutionary scientist Colin Purrington[1].

Another good read is 'Beewashing Is the New Greenwashing' by Christine Casey on the UC Davis Bee Haven blog[2].

[1] COLINPURRINGTON.COM/2019/05/HORRORS-OF-MASS-PRODUCED-BEE-HOUSES

[2] SEARCH 'BEEWASHING' ON UCANR.EDU/BLOGS/BLOGCORE

SOLITARY BEE BRICKS

And here we go, stepping into yet another red-hot conservation debate, with solitary bees in the spotlight again. Commercially produced 'bee bricks' are designed to be placed in gardens or built into walls. On England's south coast, Brighton and Hove Council recently made these bricks mandatory in all new buildings. Howls of despair about greenwash and tokenism echoed around the internet. Experts' primary concerns were that the holes were too shallow and that, after all the excitement had worn off, they also would likely be left uncleaned, risking exposing bees to predators and pathogens. Entomologist Professor Adam Hart offered perhaps the most telling comment, reminding us that 'well-meaning interventions can have unwanted consequences'.

Bee bricks are not a new idea. Traditional cob bricks and panels made from clay-rich mud and straw have long been recommended as the basis of solitary bee habitats. Purely intuitively, these appeal to me far more, but you can find more details on all of the above with an online search. Also see Resources (see pages 188–193) for a link to instructions on how to make your own cob bricks.

BUMBLEBEE NESTS AND BOXES

As mentioned on page 24, I have recently played host to a vigorous colony of White-tailed Bumblebees in my shed. We reached an accommodation; I didn't bother them, and they didn't seriously bother me. But they were big girls, with extremely bossy tendencies, even managing to see off a whole series of house-hunting Red-tailed queens. That's quite a lot of action in a smallish shed.

Their nest entrance was just a crack, almost hidden by ivy, where a wooden wall meets a stone step. The bees hovered around and sidled in and out, always hesitant to direct attention to the entrance. I spent a lot of time quietly watching them and would have given my eye teeth for a glimpse inside that nest.

You can buy, or make, bumblebee nest boxes, though again you need specialist knowledge to construct and site them. You also need to be aware of appropriate levels of observation if you are ever lucky enough to host a colony. Repeatedly opening the box would not be good for its occupants.

There are significant bumblebee populations in my garden, which tempts me to trial a nest box. The trouble is that however worthy a box might appear, your chances of getting a queen to set up home inside are quite low. You could be lucky, though, especially if you do your research. The bedding you offer is also key to success, as is a patient trial-and-error approach.

Take a look at the Resources section (see pages 188–193) for more information on buying bumblebee habitats. I also recommend Professor Dave Goulson's book *Gardening for Bumblebees*, which explores the subject in great depth and gives first-hand advice.

You can explore a compilation of artificial nest site research projects at conservationevidence.com/actions/48.

CHAPTER 6

—

GARDENING
for Bees

GARDENING FOR BEES

'Only when billions of different individual organisms make the most of every resource and opportunity they encounter, can the planet run efficiently. The greater the biodiversity, the more secure will be all life on Earth, including ourselves. Yet the way we humans are living now on Earth is sending biodiversity into a decline.'

David Attenborough, *A Life on Our Planet*

WHY GARDENING IS SO POWERFUL

When humans first gathered, and later planted to feed themselves, they already had intuitive understandings of the relationships between living organisms and their environment. Later, as the nutritional and medicinal properties of plants became better understood, we began to depend even more on good order in the natural world. Everything is interconnected.

Today, intellectually, we 'know' so much more about nature's complexities, with scientific facts and figures at our fingertips. All this, ironically, at the point when ecosystems are crashing in front of our eyes.

As a reaction to today's speedy, throwaway culture, many are taking refuge in quietly rediscovering the power of gardening, even if it's confined to a few house plants or windowsill pots. Those of us with space to cultivate are extra lucky. There are so many personal and environmental benefits of gardening, and so many positive interactions that we can bring about, not through knee-jerk responses but with patient, well-informed and mindful action.

BIODIVERSITY

We need to protect biodiversity at all costs, and many scientific studies have shown public and private gardens and allotments to be essential refuges for a rich tapestry of wildlife. Cultivated spaces are porous, interacting with surrounding environments, and when planted with a diverse range of

pollinator forage they can significantly boost both the number of species and their headcounts. (A 2004, UK National Bumblebee Nest Survey recorded an average density of 36 nests per hectare in gardens, as opposed to 11–15 nests per hectare in wild grassland settings.)

City and suburban gardens are somehow seen as inferior to country spreads, but they can be incredible engines of biodiversity. Sheffield University carried out the first large-scale analysis of biodiversity in urban gardens, finding that their soils were often better nourished than farmland and that they housed a scientifically significant diversity of plants and animals (especially allotments). Other fascinating outcomes from the study found in favour of non-native garden plants and questioned any gain from artificial bee habitats. There's a good overview of Sheffield's urban garden study (BUGS Project) online at https://tinyurl.com/4erfmadx.

Estimated at around 12 million acres, the total area of Britain's gardens outstrips the combined area of all UK nature reserves. This puts gardeners in the hot seat, giving them the ability to make a vast contribution to protecting biodiversity.

There are hurdles ahead, though, especially in times of escalating climate change. The Royal Horticultural Society's climate modelling suggests that by the 2050s UK winters are likely to be 40 per cent wetter and summers 40 per cent drier, with many more intense seasonal weather events. This is a real challenge to us all in planning and planting for sustainability (see pages 162–185).

WELLNESS

When working in my garden, muddy from top to toe, I'm often aware of being in a place of pure happiness. I'm self-taught and my ambitions often overreach reality, but I never feel that this invalidates my efforts. And nor should anyone else.

Whatever brings you to gardening and whatever your level of experience, you can relax into a therapeutic connection with nature. Let people who want to swank about their gardening credentials get on with it; just enjoy your own time among the plants you love and you will find that peaceful inner space.

Over the years, my husband Dale and I have worked on many pollinator planting projects with people for whom gardening is redemption from troubled lives, physical and mental illness, social fears or simply everyday pressures. Their stories bear witness to the healing powers of horticulture and I love their eagerness to share that path to wellness and stability, welcoming new faces into their garden family. A love of nature is one of the most powerfully uniting threads of human life.

EDUCATION

Gardens are powerful tools for lifelong learning and also a direct way for the young to discover both the pleasures of horticulture and some of the ecological conundrums they are inheriting.

I've dragged some really unwilling children into the great outdoors, but once there, they switch gear, engaging their senses and letting down their guard to become much more interactive. Once they start spotting things and asking questions, you know you've fired their interest. Gardening is already taught in some schools, but to my mind should be a non-negotiable element of every educational syllabus (even if only to help children grow up understanding where their food comes from).

Clover

EVERYTHING BEGINS WITH THE SOIL

A healthy and productive garden begins with the soil. It's not just boring brown stuff used to anchor plants – it's nature's beating heart and circulatory system, nurturing supporting life on earth. Soil itself is a living thing – a dynamic mix of organisms (from invertebrates to vital algae and fungi), decomposing organic matter (rotted-down plant, animal and microbial remains), minerals, gases and water. A single teaspoon of soil is said to contain more microbes than there are people on earth. It's potent stuff.

As all good gardeners know, it is pointless trying to cultivate anything unless the soil is in good heart. Yet, in the world of big agriculture, soils are exhausted by modern farming methods, especially the practices of monoculture (where acres of the same crop are grown repeatedly on the same land, in contrast to gentler, traditional crop rotation, which nourishes the soil) and of deep ploughing, which attempts to access richer subsoils. This results in a vicious circle in which fertilizers and pesticides are used to compensate for overworked soil and enfeebled plants lead to widespread pollution of... guess what? The soil, the air, the water table, the plants, and the creatures that feed on them.

This chemical stew is the medium in which so much of our food is grown and it is not surprising that food value indicators (such as mineral levels in green vegetables) are reportedly falling. This is often cited as one of the key reasons to favour organic produce, which, as well as tasting better, comes from resilient, well-nourished plants grown without agrichemicals on land managed to support wildlife. That's an all-round win-win, especially as yields from organically-managed land have the potential to equal, sometimes even exceed, monocultural harvests.

'60 HARVESTS'

So nutritionally depleted are soils across the world and so afflicted by erosion (laid at the door of climate change, land clearing for intensive agriculture, big engineering projects and urbanization) that in 2015, the United Nations hit the headlines estimating that we had just 60 harvests left before our soils failed to sustain the human population.

This '60 years' has been greatly disputed and probably disproved in terms of the time frame, but what's interesting is how widely it's now accepted that the clock is ticking.

It's a massive problem, which we cannot continue to brush under the carpet and it's the biggest argument I know for following organic principles, both in agriculture and in our own gardens. Which means guarding soil health, working it gently and without chemical input, and choosing what we plant. These are cornerstones in supporting plant and animal biodiversity, even in small spaces.

CLOSED NUTRIENT SYSTEMS

'Closed nutrient' is a rather grand term for a thrifty and highly effective circular approach to food production practised for centuries across countless cultures. It is especially seen in communities where subsistence living has driven the need to be completely self-sufficient. In this system, your food and your organic waste support one another, keeping nutrients intact. The resultingly productive soil is the biggest garden ally you'll ever have, helping to build a balanced ecosystem pulsing with pollinators and other wildlife.

Obviously, you have to bring new materials into a new garden, or one undergoing significant changes. Ultimately, though, the goal is to create a space where nothing is brought in and all organic matter produced is returned to the soil, enriching it and nourishing plants that you have raised yourself. That, in turn, improves both the quantity and nutritional content of food crops and the quantities and values of what the plants offer to pollinators. Another win-win.

We're a good few years off achieving this objective in our own new garden, but we are working towards it step-by-step. The first step, of course, being composting.

Soil is a living thing – a dynamic mix of organisms, decomposing matter, minerals, gases and water

COMPOSTING

Over the years, we've used different shapes and sizes of compost systems, including a garden tower system (see page 144), a sprawling heap at our London allotment and a ramshackle wooden box in the bee yard.

As we clear and reshape our large new garden, we seem destined to produce enough green waste to fuel a small biomass power station, necessitating a variety of recycling approaches, including numerous small compost heaps tucked into corners around the garden, a large-scale two-wooden-bin system that we inherited, a perfectly ordinary pedal bin in the kitchen, and some Japanese Bokashi fermented bran bins (see page 144).

Big loads of seedy weeds currently go into the council's green waste, which is hot-composted (heat means a speedy breakdown and death to most weed seeds) and sold to local gardening businesses. That's great, but I'm planning to start composting even these weeds using a hotbox system of our own, so that nothing useable ever leaves our garden.

Before a quick rundown of composting do's and don'ts and a look at some of the systems, you might want to know what we're going to do with all of this compost. Quick answer: we're going to stop digging – forever! We'll get the worms to do the work by giving them splendid layers of mulch to take down into the soil. The mulch will also do a great job of suppressing and minimizing weeds. See Resources (page 188–193) for more information on the 'No Dig' approach to gardening.

COMPOSTING PRINCIPLES

Think 'green' and 'brown' with a basic ratio of two parts 'live' green waste (nitrogenous) to one part 'dead' brown (carboniferous). A large heap of grass cuttings might be better mixed 50/50 with brown and some people recommend that ratio anyway. The compost will tell you what it needs – too much nitrogen and it will start to smell of ammonia, too much carbon and decomposition will grind to a halt. If it stinks of rotting vegetables, it's probably too wet.

Green stuff can be kitchen or garden generated; from peelings and mowings to clippings and much else besides, including weed stems (best not to include seed heads). Brown stuff can include broken eggshells, damp newspaper, tea leaves, twiggy waste, straw, chopped-up dead leaves, wood ash and shredded cardboard. Some rinsed coffee grounds will benefit the mix too. Build up in green/brown layers, but turn the heap regularly (endless advice about this is available, but once a month seems to work for us) to keep it aerated and aid decomposition.

Bruised or chopped comfrey leaves give a good extra boost, as do chopped nettles, which make a terrific composting accelerator (but add the nettles without flower/seedheads). Another super-accelerator for compost is human urine!

Raw kitchen fruit and vegetable waste can go straight into any compost system (and this is a big incentive to eat/grow organic produce). Treat citrus with caution as it's tough and too acidic to overload the compost with. I chop up and add just some of our citrus peel as well as pineapple skins and other tough stuff that takes an eternity to break down. If you have an open compost heap or bin, don't put dairy, meat/fish scraps or any cooked food into it, for the simple reason that you'll attract scavengers such as foxes and rats. Closed systems allow much more leeway in what you can recycle.

This raises the subject of heat. An active compost system is discernibly hot. The microorganisms that break waste down into compost operate effectively at temperatures of 45–70°C (113–158°F). A good heat level should destroy seeds and potential weeds, but not completely unless you are really expert. To keep an eye on the temperature, you can buy a compost thermometer.

A lot of composting is intuitive, but if your efforts are not working or it's offensively smelly and you're questioning its heat, moisture level or composition, you can find a wealth of expert advice online and in books such as The National Trust's useful little book, *Perfect Compost* (see Resources on pages 188–193 for other recommendations).

COMPOSTING SYSTEMS

A traditional composting location can begin with just a heap. Small heaps don't generate enough heat to create finished compost but are handy for starting to rot down waste that you then transfer to a larger heap, ideally not less than one cubic metre (1.3 cubic yards) in volume. To keep a heap tidy and compact, and retain heat through density, buy slatted wooden compost bins or make your own from recycled pallets.

Stepping things up a bit, you can also buy lidded tumble composters, which flip over to rotate the contents. And then you start getting into serious stuff such as insulated 'hot bins', which naturally maintain high internal temperatures. You can happily feed closed systems like these with the cooked food, dairy, raw meat and fish scraps that cause problems in open heaps or bins.

For small-space living, good options range from a simple lidded plastic bucket to compact wormeries and the Japanese Bokashi system, which we are trialling in our own garden. When we lived in London and gardened on a small terrace, we also had huge success with a compact garden tower, comprising deep planting pockets surrounding a worm-populated central tube into which you can feed lots of kitchen waste.

Now living under our kitchen sink, Bokashi is an extremely compact, two sealed-bucket system that breaks down any plant, dairy or meat/fish waste, raw or cooked. You simply alternate waste with layers of fermented bran, added to accelerate the process. Once full, you swap buckets and leave the full one alone for at least a couple of weeks before opening, using the tap in its base to draw off a nutritious liquid plant feed. The solid contents can then, in theory, go straight into soil, but we find it better adding them to the big compost bins to break down even further. The fermented bran is also a big bonus to the main heap.

The slight drawback here is that we grow/eat a lot of our own fruit and vegetables, and the amount of green waste our kitchen generates exceeds our one-on/one-off Bokashi capacity. So we've started to put some of the simple raw green stuff into a spare pedal bin that gets emptied into the open compost. We use the Bokashi mostly to deal with less easy waste, and just accept the fact that it will take a little longer. This sounds complicated when I write it down, but it really isn't. However, I am now thinking of getting a hot box as soon as possible, as an adjunct to the open compost.

The moral is to experiment and find a system that suits you and the space you have. Whichever approach you choose, you'll feel

ridiculously proud and happy if you can nourish your plantings with beautifully crumbly compost produced from your own kitchen and garden waste.

If you have nowhere to compost but like the idea of circularity, research what your local council does with the food and garden waste it collects. Increasingly, it is composted and available to buy as a finished soil dressing, from which even windowsill pots and patio container plantings can benefit.

SYMPATHETIC GARDENING

A completely closed, fully organic system is an intense undertaking, both timewise and philosophically. But even if not fully implemented, the theories behind it give us ideas and goals for improving our relationship with nature. This halfway house is what I call 'sympathetic' gardening. It's gentle, sustainable and focused on simple, traditional approaches that support plants, soil and wildlife.

Aside from composting, other elements to consider include the fact that organic systems use no artificial fertilizers or pesticides, and that any plants or seeds you bring into the garden should be sourced from credible organic production. Sadly, the majority of what's available from garden centres and many growers comes chemically pre-treated in some way, so you need to be vigilant and monitor the provenance of plants and seeds offered for sale. Other considerations include:

WATER

Water is intensely valuable and becoming ever more so. If you can access guttering downpipes, fit water butts to save and store rainwater. In dry periods, we also routinely empty dishwashing bowls, coffee-pot rinsings and other clean-ish water straight into flower beds (when we wash anything up by hand we use a mild organic soap that plants have never minded). With climate change heating everything up, it also makes sense to choose drought-resistant plants wherever possible (see page 184).

'HOME' PLANT SOURCING

Grow from seeds you have harvested from your own plants and learn how to build your plant stock using techniques such as taking cuttings and dividing existing plants (I'm good at growing from seed but definitely need to improve my skills on the other fronts). Swap plants and seeds with other people who garden organically.

COVER CROPS/GREEN MANURE

Sympathetic agricultural land management often includes the use of soil- nourishing cover crops, grown between cash crops to prevent soil erosion and later act as a 'green manure'. Gardens can benefit from this approach, too. If I have a bare patch of ground, cleared for future planting, I might well sow it directly with phacelia seeds (*Phacelia tanacetifolia*) to keep weeds at bay, provide wonderful flowering for bees and ultimately go back into the ground, either directly (although this involves digging in), cutting and leaving on the soil, or composting into mulch. Red clover, mustard and wild rocket are among many other useful plants for this. The important thing is not to leave patches of bare soil exposed for any length of time, because that's unproductive, and you'll just end up fighting weeds. Alternatively, you can mulch...

MULCHING

A mulch is a layer of material spread onto the soil. From well-rotted manure to garden compost, from straw, seaweed and cover crops to brown cardboard and leaf mould, you can use biodegradable mulches to nourish the soil, exclude weeds and protect plants from weather extremes, including heat, frost and drought. Weed-supressing mulching can clear areas of ground whenever needed, but is most effective in the growing season. Mulching to protect and nourish is best done in mid to late spring and in autumn. (But be cautious of putting deep mulches directly around new, small or ground-hugging plants, as this can lead to rot. There has to be space for air to circulate.) If you are using the 'No-Dig' method, you will also be planting directly into the mulches you create.

NATURAL PLANT FEEDS

Rich mulches go a long way to keeping plants nourished and over time continue to build up soil health. There are also many organic plant feeds on the market, or you can make your own. If you live near the sea, foraged seaweed spread onto beds is a powerful natural food and the ideal antidote to sandy soil. You can also buy liquid seaweed feed, which I swear by. If you have space to grow nettles or comfrey, use them to make feeds to enrich the soil (see opposite for a recipe).

PESTS AND DISEASES

Losing plants to pests, viruses, bacteria or fungal infection is miserable, and makes you wonder why you bothered at all. Ideally, every problem has its own timely solution, for instance ladybirds (ladybugs) will emerge to eat your greenfly and birds will help control caterpillar numbers. But you have to be a tough cookie to sit back and watch this happen and sometimes intervention is the way forward, especially in small gardens.

Fortunately, the toxic garden chemicals of old can now be replaced with natural controls. Look on organic gardening sites to help find pesticide-free solutions, which can range from picking pests off your plants to introducing physical barriers such as wool and crushed shells (to keep slugs and snails off vulnerable plants) and spraying plants with organic soap, as well as other solutions and biological controls, including companion planting and using nematodes.

Companion planting

This is a traditional method of growing different types of plant together for mutual benefit. There are numerous reasons to do this, ranging from physical support to boosting soil health, attracting beneficial insects for better pollination and, very commonly, repelling pests. One of the most common companion plants is the strong-smelling French marigold, which is often planted alongside tomatoes, potatoes, aubergines (eggplants), (bell) peppers, cucumbers and squash to protect them from whitefly and aphids.

COMFREY OR NETTLE PLANT FEED

Nettle and comfrey leaves make powerful feeds, nourishing plants with iron, nitrogen, phosphorus, potassium and many other valuable trace elements. I've yet to try them, but other leaves said to make nourishing liquid feeds include clover, bracken, borage, groundsel and strawberry.

INSTRUCTIONS

1. Put on your gardening gloves and gather a pile of nettles or comfrey. With nettles you can cut the stems and strip off the leaves. But don't cut the comfrey back, as its flowers are extremely valuable to bees – just strip a few leaves from the base of established plants.

2. Tear or roughly cut the leaves to increase their surface area and release their nutrition.

3. Transfer to a bucket (ideally one with a lid – I use one of our honey buckets, which also has a tap), filling to the brim. Push the leaves well down, adding more if there's space, then top up with just enough water to cover. Put a stone or brick on top to keep the leaves submerged and cover the bucket.

4. After a few days, the mixture will start to bubble and smell. The smell, which is pretty potent, will gather pace and in around four weeks will alert you that your plant feed is ready to use. Each brew lasts around six months, so there is no hurry to use it.

5. Dilute one part mixture with 10 parts water and feed your plants liberally with this during the growing season. Water it in at the roots or spray as a foliar feed.

6. You can re-use the same leaves by adding fresh water to make another, less potent brew. The leaf slurry ultimately makes a fine addition to your compost.

Nematodes

Beneficial nematodes are microscopic, unsegmented roundworms that you can buy as liquid drenches or sprays to deploy in the garden to control pests. If you buy some, be certain you're buying the correct nematodes to tackle the problem you have and read the instructions carefully to make sure you apply them correctly. Used well, they can be a significant help.

When to call it a day

As a footnote to all this, if something you have planted is repeatedly set back by the same problem, it's often best to call it a day and plant something else. Our Suffolk bee yard garden was an impossible place to grow tomatoes. Year after year, despite everything we tried, they developed powdery mildew. In the end we gave up – it was all too depressing. Our new Essex garden, though, is a tomato heaven.

Comfrey

CREATING NATURAL HABITATS FOR WILD BEES

Here you will find some delightfully practical and engaging adjustments that we can make to our gardens to make them attractive to pollinators and other wildlife.

But I need to start with the twin elephants in the room – 'rewilding' and 'wildflower meadows'. Both have been so fundamentally misunderstood and so rabidly preached as eco-gospel that they need to be examined from the ground up (forgive the pun).

CAN 'REWILDING' WORK IN GARDENS?

Like so many other people, I thrilled to Isabella Tree's book *Wilding*, the story of her and her husband's ambitious project at Knepp, their Sussex estate, charting the expected and unexpected outcomes of abandoning conventional land management, leaving it for nature to reclaim. But one of the formative elements in this approach is the presence of grazing animals, in Knepp's case Longhorn cattle.

When the world was younger, vast herds of wild herbivores roamed free. Their munching both stimulated and controlled plant life, and their droppings, trodden in by hooves, seeded and fertilized the land. Today, smaller herds and flocks make rewilding projects feasible on Knepp's agricultural scale, or even in a spare pasture, but really not in a domestic garden.

But this newish term, 'rewilding', has become fearsomely trendy. It is now seen as a call to leave whole gardens (and even some public spaces, although I question the financial motives here) to grow, unmanaged, entirely as they will. Absolutely fine, if you want a jungle, but please let's not call it a 'garden' any more. And there will always be significant issues with invasive plants unless the whole space is occasionally mown or eaten off.

And what would be the fate of any cultivated plants you might want to grow in this scenario? The moment you bring cultivated plants into the equation, you need to manage your garden space to maintain balance between valuable wildflowers/weeds and the more refined species that you have planted, which are easily overtaken by the wild stuff.

Planting in same-species clumps and drifts makes life easier for foraging bees

Balance is all. Blending the wild and the cultivated into a semi-wild picture offers a gentler, more biodiverse and pollinator-friendly approach than regimented gardens of yore with their green velvet lawns. But be prepared to make firm decisions about what you allow to spread and which ambitions you need to curtail through timely interventions.

Selected areas consciously left to grow wild, including lawns, grassy margins or that scruffy patch behind the shed, can be given free rein or boosted with wildflower seeds, turf or plugs. Either way, you should see heart-lifting increases in pollinators and other consequential wildlife. But in the interest of building biodiversity and the likely absence of large grazing herbivores from your front or back garden, you will need to mow or strim early in spring and then again in late summer to support wildflower growth cycles. Varying the length of the grass and changing mowing times slightly from year to year will stimulate different wildflower species.

THE WILDFLOWER MEADOW

'A meadow's serenity suggests abandon, but like a garden, establishing and maintaining it is almost entirely dependent on human management. Achieving an image of nature as we might dream it to be is not as easy as it looks... Rather than being a thoroughly low-maintenance option, as many gardeners have been led to believe, meadows need constructive hard thinking.'

CHRISTOPHER LLOYD OF GREAT DIXTER HOUSE & GARDENS,
FROM HIS CLASSIC BOOK *MEADOWS*

Perhaps no gardening concept has ever hijacked the popular gardening agenda more thoroughly than wildflower meadows. The appeal is clear, speaking to us of more innocent and carefree times. Unfortunately, in many pollinator-boosting projects with which Dale and I have been involved, money has followed sentiment. It's been heartbreaking to see our hard-won funding disappear into creating 'wildflower meadows' in completely unsuitable spaces (which, without exception, have become overgrown and abandoned within three years), rather than adopt multi-aspect pollinator plantings with the potential to thrive for decades.

Please don't think I'm against wildflower meadows; I'm as enchanted by them as anyone else and they're potentially a rich resource for wild pollinators. It's just that, as with rewilding, failure to grasp first principles can lead to poor choices and sustainability losses. A meaningful wildflower meadow requires space, expert land management – including real knowledge of soil chemistry – and specific wildflower mixes tailored to the location. And as with rewilding, its success depends on managed grazing/mowing regimes to support beneficial plant life cycles year on year. It's not 'wild' in the truest sense of the word, it's not quick, easy or cheap, and it's definitely not a plant-and-walk-away solution. If your heart is still set on one, though, expert input can mean the difference between success and failure.

Wildflower patches, however, are a very attainable goal. They work in many different (sunny) garden situations, and you can even establish them in window boxes or patio containers (although, personally, I would always plant dense clumps of flowering herbs if space is so limited).

Those packets of wildflower seeds and seed bombs that get dished out as wedding favours and to help sell 'green' products ranging from beer to shampoo, are, in my direct experience, unlikely to yield anything except disappointment. Instead, buy native wildflower seeds or plugs from reputable suppliers, ideally from someone in your own locality.

Always read up on soil requirements – most wildflowers prefer poor soils and may find 'improved' garden soil too rich.

HEDGES

A mature hedge is the land equivalent of a coral reef – a solid, yet porous structure that supports a complex ecosystem living in, on, under and around it.

For millennia, the British landscape was punctuated by densely flowering hedgerows yielding berries, fruit and nuts. But hundreds of thousands of miles of hedgerow were lost to pollinators and other wildlife as modern agriculture opened up the land after World War II. The loss to the environment, although now in some reversal, is impossible to ever fully repair.

A good hedge and its grassy margins positively burst with life; feeding and sheltering mammals, birds, invertebrates and millions of specialist organisms, including lichens, fungi and beneficial microbes. It also makes a great security barrier – nobody would tangle with wild bramble, dog rose, hawthorn or blackthorn, or more cultivated components such as pyracantha or berberis.

There are so many reasons to make space for flowering and fruiting hedges, if you can. Also consider replacing ageing wooden fences with hedges; they do take a few years to establish, so get going before the fence has fully fallen down. Professionals usually advise bare root stock hedging plants as an economical and low-input alternative to buying more established hedge plants.

DEAD HEDGING AND WOODPILES

'*Dead hedging?*' I hear you say... This is a simple, elegant concept, useful in any garden. Drawing on woodland management techniques, it uses woody prunings, fallen twigs and small branches (i.e. what would usually be waste) to create beautiful, infinitely renewable shelter and nest habitats for a variety of wild bee species, as well as beetles and other invertebrates.

A dead hedge is quick to construct, formed from two offset rows of upright branches secured into the ground, creating a space between them into which you pile brush and twigs. This builds up to a wall-like structure (usually quite low, but your choice) that can also serve as a garden barrier or divider. Dead hedging could be seen as a neater, more refined version of the woodpile, although woodpiles also provide space for bulkier waste timber such as logs and big boughs. Again, they are infinitely extendable and renewable.

As well as appealing to invertebrate life, dead hedging and woodpiles support vital mosses, lichens and fungi. Amphibians, birds and small mammals may also take advantage of both the physical shelter and the feasting opportunities offered by strong invertebrate populations.

WATER AND WATER PLANTS FOR BEES

Water in quantity is essential to honeybees, which need it to dilute their concentrated honey stores and to control their hive temperature in hot weather. Bumblebees and solitary bees mostly meet their water requirements from nectar collection, but Hairy-footed Flower Bee females (see page 90) collect water to seal their nests.

Bees of all species benefit not just from the water of a pond environment, but from the nectar and pollen-bearing plants that thrive in and around it. If you only have a small space, you can easily create a mini pond with nothing more than a dishwashing bowl. I know people who have them on balconies. The essential thing is that creatures can get in and out, and that stones, surface plants or other settling spots are in place to prevent non-swimming visitors drowning while they drink.

If a pond of any size sounds too ambitious, create the simplest water stop by putting out a shallow dish part-filled with pebbles (or better yet, shells) and let it fill with rainwater. Bees don't like clean water, so you won't need to change it; just keep it topped up in dry weather. Using a soggy area of the garden to create a marsh or bog garden planted with their specialist flora is another way of boosting biodiversity.

MUD, SAND AND SOIL

Maintaining a wet muddy patch somewhere in the garden will be invaluable to Mason bees (see page 62) and other species (including beneficial wasps) needing to gather mud to construct their nests. Making a cob brick for masonry-nesting bees is another fun bee project. Leaving a heap of builder's sand in a sunny spot or constructing a 'sandarium' (i.e. a defined sandy habitat) can also provide a safe place for burrowing bee species and other wildlife. Sunny patches or banked areas of soil, kept bare of greenery or sparsely vegetated, can attract bumblebees and solitary bees too.

See Resources on pages 188–193 for links on all of the above.

HOLLOW STEMS FOR SOLITARY BEES

Many herbaceous plants (including include sunflowers, rosebay willow herb, fennel and grasses) have hollow, pithy stems that provide natural nest sites for solitary bees. Leaving the roots in the ground, cut the stems back to around 45 cm (18 in) in winter or early spring. Ideally, leave stems from a variety of plants to offer different diameters. Some people also recommend cutting back stems to varied lengths ranging between 20–60 cm (8–24 in).

If bees do nest in the old stems, their young will emerge the following spring, so this is a two-year cycle. Some sources recommend a halfway house between leaving stems in situ and creating a formal bee house. This involves cutting and gathering hollow stems (a minimum of 15 cm /6 in long) and leaving them loose in a sheltered but potentially sunny patch at the back of a flowerbed. Bees will nest in vertical, horizontal or angled stems so there's nothing lost in trying a number of approaches.

NOWHERE TO PLANT?

Making it your mission to plant for pollinators can make you extremely resourceful. Here is my first-hand experience in identifying potential planting places and finding community support.

Green Deserts: Both urban and rural environments have 'green deserts' – places laid to lawn that look green but have little or nothing to offer pollinators. These can include golf, cricket, rugby and football clubs, athletics tracks, museum, hotel and school grounds, blocks of flats, new housing developments, science parks and many other sites. Note these places well, because they hold promise, as will many others in your locality.

Getting Permission: Get your proposition straight. You need to explain properly why pollinator plantings are so essential to the environment, the exact location you have in mind and how you will ensure that your project is safe, well planned and well maintained going forward. Take this proposal to whoever owns or manages the space you've earmarked, and you'll be amazed how often people allow you to plant. If they really engage with the idea, they may even offer a bigger or already cultivated area to improve.

Marginal Gains: I call my approach 'marginal gains', not just because I count every small victory, but because I've learned how much planting space you can create along the margins of buildings, fences, walls and other features that divide the landscape. Open up the ground along your chosen margin to create as long a bed as you can. This can be narrow (as little as 45 cm/18 in wide will do nicely), but can become a lush garden for pollinators (and other wildlife), with a mixture of woody and herbaceous perennial plantings top of the list. Dense flowering/fruiting hedges are also a great way to plant up margins.

Getting Help: Large companies have ESG (Environmental, Social and Governance) and CSR (Corporate Social Responsibility) policies. As part of these, they often seek volunteering opportunities for their staff to undertake work in the local community. It's always worth approaching companies that say they have a green agenda, but there are other powerful ways of networking too, such as talking to local social organizations (for example, the Round Table, Lions Club, Women's Institute and other community-focused groups in your area). Set out your case for planting to support pollinators and biodiversity and ask for what you need, whether that be space, plants or labour. Again, you'll be surprised by people's kindness and willingness to get involved. Local councils can be receptive to community gardening initiatives in their parks and gardens, and may even offer grants for area improvement, but don't expect this to be a quick or easy path.

CHAPTER 7

—

PLANNING &
PLANTING *for* BEES

PLANNING AND PLANTING FOR BEES

*Although by no means exhaustive – there are countless others I have
no room to mention – the lists in this section contain plants known
to significantly benefit wild bees.*

Alongside the lists, I've included some core principles for bee-
friendly plantings that I hope you will find useful, whether you are an
experienced gardener or a novice.

You can also use this chapter to find out how to 'read the label', how
the Latin names work, how to understand what you can expect from a
plant, and how to make more informed choices.

CHOOSING PLANTS FOR BEES

The plant recommendations are drawn from a wide range of resources,
from the field observations of naturalists, conservationists, horticultural
experts and bee enthusiasts to formal scientific studies. There will always
be noisy disagreements about 'the best of the best' but I've tried to reflect
the strongest consensus from the broadest possible community.

Some of the plants here particularly benefit specific bee species, but
everything listed serves at least two of the three bee groupings: solitaries,
bumblebees and honeybees. The greater majority appeals to all three.

To highlight as many plants as possible, I've tried to avoid featuring the
same ones repeatedly in different tables, so it's worth reading through all
the lists to get the broadest view.

IT'S NOT ALL ABOUT BIG GARDENS

Many of the plants listed, especially those on pages 176 and 178, work
wonderfully in containers, from pots to windowboxes. I've gardened in
many small spaces and one of the great joys of container gardening is its

infinite flexibility. Being able to control the soil conditions gives you a far wider choice of plants to grow, and with freestanding pots, you can position and reposition them strategically to make the most of sun and shade.

Also, never ignore a wall or fence that could be planted with a climber or two, also grown in pots if necessary. Vertical plantings are often overlooked but can add hugely to the forage value of any planting project, large or small.

Containers do need special attention paid to watering. Wind dries them out quickly and even heavy rain may not penetrate far enough into the soil of a densely planted pot, windowbox or hanging basket.

HOW TO USE THE LISTS

If you don't know a species I've mentioned, look it up online. Read about its preferences (think the four S's: size, soil, sun, suitability), check out specifically bee-friendly options available, and decide if you like and want to plant it. It should make you every bit as happy as it makes the bees – a garden can be both worthy and beautiful.

READ THE LABEL

Your plant choices need to be made in the context of where you are gardening – not only the space you have available but also the prevailing climate, the nature of the soil and other factors. Please don't be daunted by this – it sounds complicated, but really it's just a question of reading the plant's label and doing some simple checks that rapidly become habit.

Here are key questions to ask about any plant you think you'd like to grow. The mantra of 'right plant in the right place' is an old one, but it makes fundamental sense.

Does it prefer sun or shade?

Observe the area where you are planning to plant and work out how much sun it gets throughout the day. Most nectar-bearing plants are sun-loving, but many dapple- and even shade-tolerant plants offer good pollen.

How tall and how wide will it be when fully grown?

Make sure the space you've chosen fits the plant's long-term ambitions.

Is it invasive and liable to take over the garden?

If happy, many (especially wild) species spread like crazy. You need to know about such habits before deciding whether to let it loose. Sometimes you can curtail a plant's plans by settling it in 'not quite right' conditions. I've done this successfully in the past with Russian Vine (*Fallopia baldschuanica*), but it's a risky strategy, especially if you have limited space.

What is the consistency and chemistry of your soil?

If you are planting into containers, or into beds topped with deep no-dig mulches, don't worry too much about your soil, as you control the planting medium. Otherwise, it is important to know both your soil's consistency (ranging from heavy clay to free-draining sandy soil) and, ideally, its acidity (pH testing kits are easily available to check this).

Many plants have strong preferences. Understanding the medium in which you're asking them to grow will save you the heartbreak of seeing them fail. It will inform both your choice of plants and your approach to nurturing your soil through gentle, natural improvements.

SOME IMPORTANT GARDENING TERMS

Plants have their own rhythms, life spans and tolerances. Some flower every year, some flower for one year only. Some are species, some are varietals, some are hybrids. Here's a guide to the key terms that you'll encounter when reading about plants or checking out the labels.

FLOWERING SEASONS (northern hemisphere)

SPRING: *March, April, May*
SUMMER: *June, July, August*
AUTUMN: *September, October, November*
WINTER: *December, January, February*

HARDINESS

Gardeners talk about a plant's 'hardiness' – this is its ability to withstand tough conditions such as frost and other weather extremes. Hardy plants are a good bet for less-experienced gardeners to start with, unless you live in a divine climate.

Hardiness is often generalized from 'tender' through 'half hardy' to 'fully hardy', but there are scientific scales for those who like their facts and figures quantified. Climate change is having a profound effect on the geographical locations where certain plants can be grown, and on native plants' flowering times. This has knock-on effects for bees (see pages 49–53).

LIFE CYCLES

Annual
Blooming for a single year before dying off completely, some annuals are important to pollinators, especially as they often flower profusely. Many also shed their seeds and grow back from that seed year after year. For me annuals are the icing on the gingerbread, a quick way to boost the glamour component of any spot in the garden and/or bee forage availability.

Biennial
These are flowering plants with a two-year life cycle. They produce a base of leaves in the first year and then overwinter to flower and set seed the following year, after which they die.

Perennial
Plants with the ability to live three or more years are called perennials. These are the anchor points you need to give a garden structure and permanence.

• Herbaceous perennials die back to the ground every year, but grow back the following spring.
• Woody perennials such as trees and bushes and some climbers have woody stems that don't die back.
• Woody perennials can be deciduous or evergreen.

Deciduous

Deciduous plants lose all their leaves at some point in the year, usually during the autumn.

Evergreen

As the name suggests, evergreen plants shed and grow leaves continuously, appearing green all year round.

GENUS/SPECIES/VARIETIES/CULTIVARS

• In plant taxonomy (naming systems) the first name is the genus, for instance *Salvia*. Next in its botanical name comes its species, for instance *Salvia nemerosa*. The letters 'sp.' are shorthand for 'species' (pluralized as 'spp.').

• Many species have naturally occurring varieties, often expressed by including 'var.' in their name.

• Hybrids are cross breeds, defined as the result of cross-pollinating one specific variety of a class of plants with the pollen of another genetically different variety of that class.

• Hybrids can occur naturally but are more usually human-created cultivars. These are shown with their name in inverted commas, e.g. *Salvia nemorosa* 'Ostfriesland'. The word 'cultivar' is commonly held to be an abbreviation of 'cultivated variety'.

• Some cultivars such as Geranium 'Rozanne' prove to be bee-magnets, but far too many of these novel plants are useless to pollinators. The so-called 'Cultivar Conundrum' is well explained on the Xerces Society website xerces.org/blog/cultivar-conundrum.

NATIVE OR NON-NATIVE?

This is a contentious area, not least in the niceties of definition – at what point, for instance, can a long-naturalized plant be seen as native?

Wild bee species, especially solitaries, are dependent on native flora (especially wildflowers) – far more so than honeybees and some bumblebees. It's vital that these native wild plants remain available to them.

But climate change is now creating extreme events, forcing us to look at more hot/cold/drought-resistant pollinator plantings. Bee-friendly plants from North America, the Middle East, Africa, Asia and the Antipodes are already thriving far from their places of origin. Many have already been in British gardens for hundreds of years.

'Nativists' rail against the tide of foreign flora and, yes, it's not ideal in ecological terms – moving plants or animals around the globe always creates unforeseen consequences. But at this point it is hard to imagine turning the clock back. (See recent research by the Royal Horticultural Society: rhs.org.uk/wildlife/native-and-non-native-plants-for-pollinators.)

CORE PRINCIPLES OF BEE-FRIENDLY PLANTINGS

PLANT IN CLUMPS AND DRIFTS

Mimic nature by planting in good-sized same-species clumps, or create corridors of a particular plant with 'drifts' nestled alongside drifts of other species. If you are container planting, don't mix it up too much – I tend only to plant one type of plant per container. Grouping like this saves bees energy, especially those that forage on just a single type of flower at a time.

GARDENING REALITY CHECK

Your gardening will be so much more rewarding if your plants thrive. Most of us are chronically short of time, so it makes sense for the foundations of your pollinator garden to consist of robust, low-maintenance plants that provide excellent ground coverage, cutting down the need to weed. Plant trees, climbers and plenty of different shrubs (if you have space) plus dense clumps or drifts of long-flowering drought-resistant perennials. Garnish with wild or cultivated annuals and biennials. Barring big trees, most of this can also be accomplished with container gardening.

My personal inspirations for this lush, relaxed, semi-wild style of gardening include Dutch landscape designer Piet Oudolf and two iconic British gardeners, Beth Chatto and Christopher Lloyd (see pages 188–193).

LOVE WEEDS

By changing your views on 'weeds' such as dandelions and thistles and accepting the fact that a wildlife/pollinator-friendly garden benefits from a managed combination of wild and cultivated plant species, you will start to see the space differently, in a less regimented form. Mow infrequently to allow small species such as daisies and clover to populate lawn areas and leave some shaggy margins from early spring to late summer, only cutting them 2–3 times a year, typically, March (possibly August) and October. A good way to manage valuable but invasive wild species is by cutting off the flowering heads immediately after they've flowered and before they set seed.

PLANT SEQUENTIALLY FOR ALL FOUR SEASONS

There will be some bees active at almost every time of year, especially as climate change creates warmer winters. Provide forage through all four seasons by planting sequentially, so that as one wave of floral resources dies back, another comes into bloom. The period from late autumn through to early spring is a particularly useful time to ensure forage availability. Another sensitive point is early summer, when there is often a lull in flowering cycles, known as the 'June gap'.

GO CHEMICAL FREE

Nowadays there are so many eco-alternatives to the toxic pesticides and fertilizers that used to lurk in every garden shed. Read up on organic methods and follow experts on social media for practical approaches. Even if you can't bring yourself to go 100 per cent agrichemical free at first, a start is way better than nothing. Whenever possible, buy seeds, plants and peat free potting composts (always peat-free) from organic sources, to ensure they haven't been pre-treated with chemicals (see page 138).

CHOOSE SIMPLE FLOWER FORMS

So many plants have been 'improved' by breeders developing new forms, colours, sizes and so on. Occasionally these can be advantageous to bees, but mostly there's a significant (or total) loss of forage value.

For instance, miles removed from its original open-faced daisy form, a sassy pom-pom dahlia has no more to offer bees than a multi-petalled rose. Many other plants suffer the same fate when bred far away from their original forms. Stick as close as you can to the wild forms, with simple, original flower shapes.

FAVOUR PURPLES AND BLUES

If you are wondering why so many of the plants featured in this book are purple or blue, it's no coincidence. Purple, blue and white flowers are extremely visible and especially attractive to bees, which see from yellow, blue and green right into the ultraviolet (UV) light scale (see pages 28–29). A bee-focused garden typically has a strong showing of these colours.

20 BUSHES & TREES FOR BEES

Essential to so many species of bee, bushes and trees tend to have fairly brief flowering times, but offer a feast while in bloom. They also provide important habitat for countless species.

COMMON NAME	LATIN NAME	FLOWERING PERIOD
Blackberry (*Bramble*)	*Rubus fruiticosus*	*May to September*
Apple	*Malus pumila (or domestica), Malus sylvestris Crab Apple (simple form not double flowered)*	*April to May*
Currants	*Ribes sanguinem Flowering currant, R. nigrum Blackcurrant, R. rubrum Redcurrant/Whitecurrant*	*April to May*
Hawthorn	*Crataegus spp. including: C. monogyna Hawthorn, C. Laevigata Midland Hawthorn*	*May to June*
Cherry (*not double flowered*)	*Prunus cerasus Sour Cherry, P. padus Wild Cherry, P. avium Bird/Wild Cherry P. × yedoensis Yoshino Cherry, P. spinosa Blackthorn*	*April to May*
Wild Rose	*Rosa rugibinosa Sweet Briar, Eglantine, R. rugosa Beach Rose, R. canina Dog Rose, R. spinossima Burnet/Scottish Rose*	*Mainly June to July*
Alder Tree	*Alnus glutinosa Common Black Alder, A. cordata Italian Alder*	*Catkins January to March / Catkins February to April*
Willow (*Sallow*) **Bush/Tree/ Hedge**	*Salix spp. including: Salix caprea Goat/Pussy Willow or Sallow, S. babylonica Weeping Willow, S. cinerea Grey Willow*	*Catkins February to March, depending on species*
Chestnut Tree	*Aesculus hippocastanum Horse Chestnut, Castanea sativa Sweet Chestnut*	*Flowers in May Catkins in July*
Holly Bush/ Tree/Hedge	*Ilex spp. including: I. aquifolium Holly, I. opaca American Holly, I. glabra Inberry/ Gallberry, I. crenata Japanese Boxleaf Holly*	*May to June*

COMMON NAME	LATIN NAME	FLOWERING PERIOD
Maple Tree	*Acer spp. including: A. campestre, Field Maple, A. rubrum Canadian/Red Maple*	*April to May*
Robinia *(False Acacia)* **Tree**	*Robinia Pseudoacacia Black Locust*	*May to June*
Lime Tree	*Tilia spp including: T. cordata Small leaved Lime, T. platyphyllos Large leaved Lime, T. maximowicziana Japanese Lime, Tilia × europeaea*	*June to July*
Gorse Bush/ Hedge	*Ulex europaeus*	*February to June*
Heather Bush	*Erica spp. and Calluna spp. including:*	
	C. vulgaris Ling,	*August to October*
	E. cinerea Bell,	*March to September*
	E. tetralix Cross Leaf,	*June to September*
	E. carnea Autumn/Winter Heather	*January to April*
Broom Bush/Hedge	*Cytisus spp. including: C. scoparius (wild and cultivated), C. multiflorus Portugese Broom*	*May to June*
Privet Bush/Tree/ Hedge	*Ligustrum spp. including: L. ovalifolium Garden Privet, L. vulgare Wild Privet*	*August to September*
Hebe Bush/ Hedge *Choose flowering species only*	*Hebe spp. including:*	
	H. brachysiphon Short Tubed Hebe	*July to August*
	H. hulkeana New Zealand Lilac	*April to May*
	H. 'Autumn Glory' (autumn flowering)	*July to October*
Buddleja Bush/Tree	*Buddleja spp. including: B. globosa Orange Ball Tree, B. davidii (wild and cultivated), B. × weyeriana*	*May to October*
Cotoneaster Bush/Tree/ Hedge	*Cotoneaster spp. including:*	*May to July*
	C. lucidus Hedge Cotoneaster,	
	C. adpresssus Creeping Cotoneaster,	
	C. horizontalis Wall Cotoneaster,	
	C. frigidus Himalayan Cotoneaster Tree	*June to July*

20 WILDFLOWERS THAT
ARE IMPORTANT TO BEES

*Although essentially wild, most of these flowers can also be cultivated
in gardens. But be aware that many have a tendency to be invasive,
so do your research before planting or deciding whether
to leave existing specimens in place.*

COMMON NAME	LATIN NAME	FLOWERING PERIOD
Dandelions	*Taraxacum officinale Common Dandelion*	*May to October*
Clovers	*Trifolium spp. including: T. pratense Red Clover*	*May to October*
	T. repens White or Dutch Clover,	*June to September*
	T. hybrida Alsike Clover,	*April to October*
	Melilotus spp. Sweet Clover	*May to September*
Trefoil	*Lotus corniculatus Bird's-foot, Trefoil*	*May to September*
	Trifolium dubium Lesser Trefoil	*May to June*
Willow Herb/ Weed	*Chamerion angustifolium, Rosebay Willow Herb,*	*June to September*
	Epilobium hirsutum Hairy Willow Weed	*July to August*
Deadnettle	*Lamium spp. including:*	
	L. album White Deadnettle,	*March to November*
	L. purpureum Red Deadnettle,	*March to November*
	L. maculatum Spotted Deadnettle	*May to June*
Fleabane	*Pilicaria dysenterica Common Fleabane*	*July to September*
Wood Sage	*Teucrium scorodonia*	*July to September*
Teasels	*Dipsacus spp.*	*July to August*
Sea Kale	*Crambe maritima, C. cordifolia*	*May to July*
Sea Lavender	*Limonium vulgare*	*July*
Common Mallow	*Malva sylvestris*	*June to October*

COMMON NAME	LATIN NAME	FLOWERING PERIOD
Bistort	*Persicaria bistorta Common Bistort,*	*June to September*
	Persicaria maculosa Redshank	*June to October*
Knapweeds	*Centaurea spp. including: C. nigra Common*	*June to September*
	Knapweed, C. scabiosa Greater Knapweed	
Vetches	*Vicia spp. including: Vicia sativa Common*	
	Vetch,	*May to September*
	Anthyllis vulneraria Kidney Vetch,	*June to September*
	Lathyrus pratensis Meadow Vetchling,	*May to August*
	Hippocrepis comosa Horseshoe Vetch	*May to July*
Bristly Ox Tongue	*Helminthotheca echioides*	*June to November*
Hawksbeard	*Crepis spp. including:*	
	C. capillaris Smooth Hawksbeard,	*June to September*
	C. vesicaria Beaked Hawksbeard,	*May to July*
	C. biennis Rough Hawksbeard	*July to September*
Ground Ivy	*Glechoma hederacea (this is a member*	*March to July*
	of the mint family, so not an ivy at all!)	
Selfheal	*Prunella vulgaris*	*June to October*
Figworts	*Scrophularia spp. including: S. nodosa*	*July to September*
Wild Umbellifers	*Parsley/carrot family, including:*	
	Daucus carota Queen Anne's Lace,	*June to August*
	Anthriscus sylvestris Cow Parsley,	*May to June*
	Smyrnium olusatrum Alexanders,	*April to June*
	Angelica archangelica Angelica,	*June to July*
	Pastinaca sativa Wild Parsnip,	*June to September*
	Heracleum sphondylium Hogweed	*May to August*

20 TOP MEDICINAL
& KITCHEN HERBS FOR BEES

These herbs offer powerful medicinal properties and, in many cases,
flavourful additions to food. But you need to let your herbs flower if
they are to be useful to the bees, so resist the temptation to keep pinching
all the tops off. I plant some for the kitchen and some for the bees.

COMMON NAME	LATIN NAME	FLOWERING PERIOD
Rosemary	*Salvia rosmarinus (formerly Rosmarinus officinalis)*	*April to June*
Mint	*Mentha spp. including: Mentha × piperita Peppermint/Mentha spicata Spearmint, Pycnanthemum spp. Mountain Mints*	*August to September* *Late summer*
Basil	*Osimum spp. including: O. tenuiflorum Holy Basil/Tulsi, O. basilicum var. minimum Greek Basil, O. basilicum var. thyrsiflora Thai Basil*	*July to September*
Nepeta/Catmint	*Nepeta spp. including: N. cateria Catmint, N. × fassenii Garden Catmint, N. racemose Calamintha nepeta Lesser Calamint*	*June to September* *July to September*
Comfrey	*Symphytum officinale*	*May to July*
Hyssop	*Hyssopus officianalis*	*July to September*
Fennel	*Foeniculum vulgare Common Fennel, F. vulgare var. dulce Sweet Fennel*	*July to August* *June to August*
Borage	*Borago officinalis*	*April to October*
Calendula	*Calendula officinalis Pot Marigold*	*June to September*
Chamomile	*Chamaemelum nobile Roman Chamomile, Matricaria chamomilla German Chamomile, Anthemis arvensis Corn Chamomile*	*June to August* *June to July* *June to September*

COMMON NAME	LATIN NAME	FLOWERING PERIOD
Bee Balm *(Bergamot)*	*Monarda spp. including: M. punctata Spotted Bee Balm, M. didyma Scarlet Bee Balm, M. fistulosa Wild Bergamot*	*July to September*
Dill	*Anethum graveolens*	*May to July*
Lavender	*Lavandula spp. including: L. angustifolia English Lavender, L. × intermedia 'Hidcote Giant', L. 'Edelweiss'*	*June to August*
Lemon Balm	*Melissa officinalis*	*June to September*
Eupatorium	*Eupatorium cannabinum Hemp Agrimony, Eupatorium perfoliatum Boneset*	*July to September* *August to September*
Oregano/ Marjoram	*Origanum spp. including: O. vulgare Wild Marjoram, O. majorana Sweet Marjoram, O. syriacum Syrian Oregano, O. onites Cretan Oregano*	*June to September* *May to July* *July to September*
Sage	*Salvia officinalis*	*June to August*
Thyme	*Thymus spp. including: T. polytrichus Wild Thyme, T. vulgaris Garden Thyme, T. capitatus Conehead Thyme, T. × citriodorus Lemon Thyme*	*May to August*
Yarrow	*Achillea millefolium Common Yarrow Achillea tomentosa Woolly Yarrow*	*June to September*
Coriander	*Coriandrum sativum*	*Summer*

20 GARDEN FLOWERS THAT ARE IMPORTANT TO BEES

While many of the species here are wild, they happily grow as garden flowers too. Sometimes there's too much choice, especially if a species has masses of varieties or cultivars, so go online and check their bee-friendly credentials before buying.

KEY

Bee: Choose species / varieties / cultivars specifically listed as bee-friendly
Flower: Sizes / colours / habits to suit many gardening situations including containers

COMMON NAME	LATIN NAME	FLOWERING PERIOD
Aster	*Aster novi-belgii New York Aster, A. tripolium Sea Aster, A. × frikartii 'Mönch' Michaelmas Daisy, Symphyotrichum cordifolium Blue Wood Aster, Eurybia divaricate White Wood Aster, A. lateriflorus Calico Aster, Also: Chamomiles (same family) inc. Anthemis tinctoria*	*Summer into autumn*
Salvia	*Salvia Nemorosa Woodland Sage, S. × sylvestris 'Caradonna', S. 'Amistad', S. sclarea Clary Sage, S. viridis Crested Sage, S. yangii (formerly Perovskia atriplicifolia) Russian Sage, S. Rosmarinus (formerly Rosmarinus officinalis) Rosemary*	*Spring into autumn*
Hardy Geranium *(Cranesbill or True Geranium)**	*Geranium 'Rozanne', Geranium 'Spinners' Geranium maculatum Spotted Cranesbill, G. maculatum 'Beth Chatto', G. robertianum Herb Robert, G. sanguineum var. striatum Striped Bloody Cranesbill, G. pratense Meadow Cranesbill, G. pratense 'Striatum' and 'Spinners'*	*Spring into autumn*
Lungwort	*Pulmonaria officinalis Common Lungwort, P. officinalis 'Opal', P. rubra var albocorollata*	*Early spring into early summer*

* (Not to be confused with Pelargonium 'Geraniums')

COMMON NAME	LATIN NAME	FLOWERING PERIOD
Stachys	*Stachys officinalis Betony, S. sylvatica Hedge Woundwort, S. byzantina Lamb's Ear, S. 'Hummelo'*	*Summer*
Achillea	*Achillea millefolium Common Yarrow, A. millefolium 'Proa', A. clypeolata Balkan Yarrow, A. filipendulina 'Cloth of Gold', Fern Leaf Yarrow, A. ptarmica 'The Pearl', A. taygetea Egyptian Yarrow, A. tomentosa Woolly Yarrow*	*Summer into autumn*
Bellflower	*Campanula rotundifolia Harebells (sometimes called Scottish Bluebells), C. glomerata Clustered Bellflower, C. carpatica Carpathian Bellflower, C. medium Canterbury Bells, C. trachelium Nettle-leaved Bellflower, C. rapunculus Rampions*	*Summer into autumn*
Cornflower	*Centaurea cyanus Annual Wild Cornflower, C. montana Perennial Mountain Cornflower, C. nigra Knapweed, C. scabiosa Greater Knapweed, C. moschata Sweet Sultan*	*Summer to autumn*
Echium	*Echium vulgare Viper's Bugloss, E. vulgare 'Blue Bedder', E. pininana Giant/Tree Echium*	*Early summer into autumn*
Foxglove	*Digitalis purpurea Native Foxglove, D. lanata Woolly Foxglove, D. parviflora Small-flowered Foxglove*	*Spring into early summer*
Monk's Hood Aconitum	*Aconitum napellus, A. napellus henryi Sparks variety, A. carmichaelii*	*Summer*
Hellebore Choose simple, bee-accessible flower forms	*Helleborus niger Christmas Rose, H. orientalis Lenten Rose, H. viridis Green Hellebore, H. foetidus Stinking Hellebore, H. × hybridus, H. × sahinii 'Winterbells', H. × ballardiae*	*December to April*

COMMON NAME	LATIN NAME	FLOWERING PERIOD
Scabious/Knautia	*Centaurea scabiosa Greater Knapweed,* *Knautia Macedonia Macedonian Knapweed,* *K. arvensis Field Scabious*	*Summer into autumn*
Sedum/Stonecrop	*Sedum spectabile Ice Plant, S. spectabile* *'Autumn Joy', S. telephium 'Matrona',* *S. spurium, S. album*	*Spring into autumn*
Thistle Family	*Echinops spp. Globe Thistle including:* *E. sphaerocephalus Glandular Globe Thistle,* *E. bannaticus Hungaria Globe Thistle,* *E. ritro 'Veitch's Blue', Eryngium maritimum* *Wild Sea Holly, E. planum Flat Sea Holly, E.* *zabelii 'Big Blue', E. × tripartitum,* *E. alpinum Alpine Sea Holly, E. giganteum,* *Cirsium rivulare 'Atropurpureum' Plume* *Thistle, C. vulgare Spear Thistle,* *C. dissectum Marsh Thistle, Silybum* *marianum Blessed Milk Thistle*	*Summer into autumn*
Verbena	*Verbena bonariensis Argentinian Vervain,* *V. rigida Slender Vervain, V. speciosa* *'Imagination' Trailing Verbena, V. hybrida* *'Peaches and Cream'*	*Summer into autumn*
Veronica	*Veronica longifolia Garden Speedwell,* *V. spicata Spiked Speedwell, V. chamaedrys* *Wild Speedwell*	*Spring to autumn*
Agastache	*Agastache foeniculum Anise Hyssop,* *A. 'Blue Boa', A. 'Black Adder',* *A. rugosa Korean Mint*	*Summer into autumn*
Violets	*Viola odorata Sweet Violet, V. riviana* *purpurea Common Dog Violet, V. cornuta* *Horned Violet*	*Winter into early* *summer*
Anemone	*Anemone nemorosa Wood Anemone,* *A. blanda Winter Windflower,* *A. coronaria Garden Anemone*	*Late winter into* *spring*

10 TOP GARDEN
CROPS FOR BEES

*So many of our food crops are pollinated by bees. With some, such as
brassicas, we only eat the leaves, harvesting them before the plants
flower. But if we allow some of these to bloom too, we can feed
bees and produce seed for the following year.*

COMMON NAME	LATIN NAME	FLOWERING PERIOD
Artichokes & **Cardoons**	*Cynara cardunculus Cardoon, C. cardunculus var. scolymus Artichoke*	*June to September*
Turnip	*Brassica rapa rapa White Turnip*	*Depends on sowing time*
Kale	*Brassica oleracea (Acephala Group)*	*Spring*
Blueberry	*Vaccinium spp. including: V. myrtillus European Blueberry/Bilberry*	*June to July*
Radish	*Raphanus spp.*	*Depends on sowing time*
Strawberry	*Fragaria spp.*	*May/June*
Bean & **Pea Family**	*Phaseolus spp., Pisum sativum Peas, Cicer arietinum Chickpeas, Vicia faba Broad Bean*	*Depends on sowing time*
Onion Family	*Allium spp. including: A. cepa Onion A. porrum Leek, A. schoenoprasum Chives, A. siculum Sicilian Honey Garlic*	*May to August*
Tomatoes	*Solanum lycopersicum*	*Summer*
Squash Family	*Cucurbitae spp. including: Courgette, Marrow, Pumpkin etc.*	*June to August*

10 GOOD CLIMBERS, SCRAMBLERS & RAMBLERS

Use any available walls and fences to boost the floral density available to pollinators.

COMMON NAME	LATIN NAME	FLOWERING PERIOD
Honeysuckle	*Lonicera spp.,*	
	Lonicera periclymenum,	*July to September*
	L. sempervirens Trumpet Honeysuckle,	*April to July*
	L. japonica Japanese Honeysuckle,	*April to August*
	L. fragrantissima Winter Honeysuckle	*December to March*
Climbing and Rambling Roses	*Rosa spp. including:*	***Climbers:*** *Summer*
	Climbing: R. filipes 'Kiftsgate', R. moschata,	*into autumn (repeat*
	R. polyantha 'Grandiflora',	*flowering)*
	Rambling: R. Kew Rambler, R. Rambling	***Ramblers:*** *June to*
	Rector, R. Bobbie James	*July (one flowering)*
Boston Ivy	*Parthenocissus tricuspidata*	*June to August*
Flowering Ivy	*Hedera helix*	*September to November*
	Hedera colchica Persian Ivy	*October to December*
Clematis *Choose varieties named as bee-friendly*	*Clematis spp. including:* *C. tangutica Golden Clematis,* *C. cirrhosa Winter Jasmine* *(especially 'Freckles')*	*July to September* *December to March*
Black-eyed Susan	*Thunbergia alata*	*June to October*
Passiflora	*Passiflora spp., P. incarnata True,* *Passionflower, P. caerulea Common* *Passionflower, P. edulis Passion Fruit*	*June to September*
Jasmine	*Jasmimum officinale Common Jasmine,*	*June to August*
	J. nudiflorum Winter Jasmine	*December to April*
Nasturtium	*Tropaeolum majus*	*July to September*
Climbing Hydrangea	*Hydrangea anomala petiolaris*	*June to July*

10 BEE PLANTS FOR DAMP AREAS
& MARSH/POND MARGINS

Plants that enjoy constant access to water are often extremely
productive and attractive to bees.

COMMON NAME	LATIN NAME	FLOWERING PERIOD
Watercress	*Nasturtium officinale*	*March to October*
Marsh Marigold	*Caltha palustris*	*February to June*
Water Mint	*Mentha aquatica*	*July to October*
Marsh Mallow	*Althaea officinalis*	*July to September*
Devil's Bit Scabious	*Succisa pratensis*	*June to September*
Water Avens	*Geum rivale*	*May to September*
Water Figwort	*Scrophularia auriculata*	*June to September*
Skullcap	*Scutellaria galericulata Common Skullcap, Scutellaria lateriflora Blue Skullcap*	*June to September*
Iris	*Iris pseudacorus Yellow Flag Iris, Iris versicolor Blue Flag Iris, Scutellaria lateriflora Blue Skullcap*	*May to August* *May to June*
Loosestrife	*Lythrum salicaria Purple Loosestrife, Lysimachia vulgaris Yellow Loosestrife (NB both can be invasive), Iris versicolor Blue Flag Iris, Scutellaria lateriflora Blue Skullcap*	*June to August* *June to September*

10 DROUGHT-TOLERANT BEE PLANTS

As climate change grows more pronounced, so it becomes more important to choose plants able to tolerate dry conditions once they are established.

COMMON NAME	LATIN NAME	FLOWERING PERIOD
Helenium (Sneezeweed)	Helenium spp.	July to September
Echinacea	Echinacea spp.	June to September
Gaillardia (Blanketflower)	Gaillardia spp.	June to September
Red Campion	Silene dioica	April to July
Agastache	Agastache foeniculum Anise Hyssop	June to September
Coreopsis (Tickseed)	Coreopsis spp.	June to September
Creeping Rosemary	Salvia rosmarinus (formerly Rosmarinus officinalis) Prostratus Group	Spring and summer
Goldenrod	Solidago spp. S. canadensis	August to September
Liatris (Blazing Star)	Liatris spicata	August to September
Rudbeckia	Rudbeckia spp., R. fulgida var. sullivantii 'Goldsturm', R. hirta Black-eyed Susan	July to October

LATE/EARLY FORAGE:
10 ADDITIONAL IDEAS

Planting forage to feed bees into winter and early spring is vitally important. These plants are additional to the early/late flowering species mentioned on the previous pages.

COMMON NAME	LATIN NAME	FLOWERING PERIOD
Mahonia	*Mahonia spp., Mahonia × media, M. aquifolium Oregon Grape*	*November to March*
Japanese Quince	*Chaenomeles japonica*	*February to April*
Winter Honeysuckle	*Lonicera fragrantissima*	*November to February*
Wallflowers	*Erysimum spp. including E. cheiranthus, E. bicolor 'Bowles Mauve' Perennial wallflower*	*February to May* *All year*
Hellebores	*Helleborus spp., Choose simple single flower varieties*	*December to April, according to plants chosen*
Bulbs, including **Crocus**	*Crocus spp. including: C. vernus C. sativus*	*Autumn/winter/spring flowering, according to plants chosen*
Grape Hyacinth	*Muscari spp. including: Muscari neglectum Common Grape Hyacinth*	*April/May*
Snowdrop	*Galanthus spp. / Choose single-flowered species such as Galanthus nivalis*	*January to March*
Winter Aconite	*Eranthis hyemalis*	*February to March*
Primula	*Primula vulgaris Common Primula, P. veris Cowslip, P. elatior Oxlip*	*December to May April to May*
Wintersweet *(Japanese Allspice)*	*Chimonanthus praecox*	*December to February*
Wild Strawberry Tree	*Arbutus unedo*	*September to November*

CHAPTER 8

—

RESOURCES

RESOURCES

This section gives a wide range of starting points, whether you want to delve deeper into the science, find a field guide for bee identification, support a charity, take some courses, or source products from recommended suppliers.

I've tried to avoid listing obviously honeybee-centric resources because now you have read this book, you will hopefully know that 'saving the bees' is not about boosting hived honeybee numbers – they are already at record highs (see page 12). While we, of course, need to be extremely worried about what the future holds for all pollinating insects, this book is about understanding and supporting our wild bees.

And it's important for me to say, again, that even just knowing more about wild bees is a powerful act of support. But hopefully this will lead you to follow your own path to more ways in which you can help.

If you have both space and the desire to plant, that's wonderful. But if you have nowhere of your own to garden, there are many community and charity planting projects where a few hours' input or some financial support will make an important difference. If you can't find a local group, take a look around your area for green spaces that you might be able to borrow to start your own project (see page 162–185 for my first-hand advice on finding places to plant).

I hope you enjoy the resources I've listed here, and that they will help you either build more knowledge around subjects I've raised, or spin off into surrounding topics that have sparked your interest.

BIBLIOGRAPHY/RECOMMENDED READING

These are some of the titles from my own library that have been important in researching this book. They will also be of real interest to anyone wanting to read more about the topics I've covered.

SCIENCE AND IDENTIFICATION

General

Field Guide to the Bees of Great Britain and Ireland (Steven Falk)
ISBN 978 1 4729 6705 3

The Bees in Your Backyard – A Guide to North America's Bees (Joseph S. Wilson & Olivia Messinger Carril)
ISBN 978 0 6911 6077 1

Bumblebees

Bumblebees – An Introduction (Nikki Gammans, Richard Comont, S.C. Morgan, Gill Perkins)
ISBN 978 0 9957 7390 5

Bumblebees – The Natural History & Identification of the Species Found in Britain (Ted Benton)
ISBN 978 0 0071 7450 8

Solitary Bees

Solitary Bees (Ted Benton)
ISBN 978 1 7842 7088 9

The Solitary Bees: Biology, Evolution, Conservation (Bryan N. Danforth)
ISBN 978 0 6911 6898 2

Wild Honeybees

The Lives of Bees – The Untold Story of the Honey Bee in the Wild (Thomas D. Seeley)
ISBN 978 0 6911 6676 6

The Biology of The Honey Bee (Mark L. Winston)
ISBN 978 0 6740 7409 5

Wasps

Endless Forms: The Secret World of Wasps (Sierian Summer)
ISBN 978 0 0083 9447 9

Bees and The Environment

The Garden Jungle (Dave Goulson)
ISBN 978 1 7873 3135 8

Pollinators and Pollination: Nature and Society (Jeff Ollerton)
ISBN 978 1 7842 7228 9

Silent World: Averting the Insect Apocalypse (Dave Goulson)
ISBN 978 1 7873 3334 5

Bee Intelligence

The Mind of a Bee (Lars Chittka)
ISBN 978 0 6911 8047 2

Plant Life/Ecology

How Plants Work
(Stephen Blackmore)
ISBN 978 1 7824 0697 6

Weeds (Richard Mabey)
ISBN 978 1 8466 8076 2

Wilding (Isabella Tree)
ISBN 978 1 5098 0510 5

A Life on Our Planet
(David Attenborough)
ISBN 978 1 5291 0829 3

Gardening: General and Situational

Organic Gardening: The Natural No-Dig Way (Charles Dowding)
ISBN 978 0 8578 4089 9

Grow Easy: Organic Crops for Pots and Small Plots (Anna Greenland)
ISBN 978 1 7842 735 2

Meadows (Christopher Lloyd)
ISBN 978 1 8440 3066 8

Drought-resistant Planting (Beth Chatto) ISBN 978 0 7112 3811 4

Grow A Living Wall: Create Vertical Gardens with Purpose
(Shawna Coronado)
ISBN 978 1 5918 6624 4

The Rooftop Growing Guide
(Annie Novak)
ISBN 978 1 6077 4708 6

The Wildlife Pond Book: Create Your Own Pond Paradise for Wildlife
(Jules Howard)
ISBN 978 1 4729 5832 7

How to Make and Use Compost: The Ultimate Guide (Nicky Scott)
ISBN 978 1 9003 2259 1

Plants for Bees
(W. D. Kirk and F. N. Howes)
ISBN 978 0 8609 8271 5

100 Plants to Feed the Bees
(Xerces Society)
ISBN 978 1 6121 2701 9

ONLINE RESOURCES

Bee Information and Research

BEES, WASPS & ANTS RECORDING SOCIETY (BWARS): bwars.com

BUGLIFE: buglife.org.uk

BUMBLEBEE CONSERVATION TRUST: bumblebeeconservation.org

STEVEN FALK, ENTOMOLOGIST/ BEE EXPERT: researchgate.net/ profile/Steven-Falk-2

GLOBAL BIODIVERSITY
INFORMATION FACILITY (GBIF):
gbif.org

NBN ATLAS: nbnatlas.org

QUEEN MARY UNIVERSITY OF
LONDON: qmul.ac.uk
(search 'bees')

SUSSEX UNIVERSITY, GOULSON
LAB: sussex.ac.uk/lifesci/
goulsonlab/

SHEFFIELD UNIVERSITY:
sheffield.ac.uk (search 'bees')

UK CENTRE FOR ECOLOGY AND
HYDROLOGY: ceh.ac.uk/our-
science/projects/uk-pollinator-
monitoring-scheme

THE WILDLIFE TRUSTS:
wildlifetrusts.org

NATIVE BEE INVENTORY AND
MONITORING (USA): usgs.gov/
centers/eesc/science/native-bee-
inventory-and-monitoring-lab

THE PROCEEDINGS OF THE
NATIONAL ACADEMY OF
SCIENCES (USA): pnas.org
(search 'bees')

US NATIVE BEES (US):
usnativebees.com

THE XERCES SOCIETY FOR
INVERTEBRATE CONSERVATION
(USA): xerces.org

Gardening and the Environment

CPRE, THE COUNTRYSIDE
CHARITY: cpre.org.uk

EAT THE WEEDS:
eattheweeds.com

THE KEW REPORT: kew.org/
science/state-of-the-worlds-
plants-and-fungi

PLANTLIFE: plantlife.
love-wildflowers.org.uk

ROYAL HORTICULTURAL
SOCIETY: rhs.org.uk

ROYAL SOCIETY FOR THE
PROTECTION OF BIRDS:
rspb.org.uk/our-work/state-
of-nature-report/

THE SOIL ASSOCIATION:
soilassociation.org

AMERICAN HORTICULTURAL
SOCIETY (USA): ahsgardening.org/
gardening-resources/sustainable-
gardening/

Citizen Science Projects

BEES, WASPS & ANTS
RECORDING SOCIETY (BWARS):
bwars.com/content/observations

DATABASE OF POLLINATORS
INTERACTIONS (DOPI):
dopi.org.uk/contribute

FRIENDS OF THE EARTH:
friendsoftheearth.uk/nature/bee-surveys-record-bees-and-help-science

NATIONAL GEOGRAPHIC:
education.nationalgeographic.org/resource/citizen-science-projects

UK CENTRE FOR ECOLOGY AND HYDROLOGY: ceh.ac.uk/citizen-science

UK POLLINATOR MONITORING SCHEME: ukpoms.org.uk

THE WILDLIFE TRUSTS: wildlifetrusts.org/citizen-science

THE BEE CONSERVANCY (USA): thebeeconservancy.org/citizen-community-science-for-bees/

THE XERCES SOCIETY (USA): xerces.org/community-science

Allotments and Community Gardening

LOCAL ALLOTMENT APPLICATIONS: gov.uk/apply-allotment

ROYAL HORTICULTURAL SOCIETY: rhs.org.uk/get-involved/community-gardening/find-a-group

SOCIAL FARMS AND GARDENS: farmgarden.org.uk/your-area

AMERICAN COMMUNITY GARDENING ASSOCIATION (US): communitygarden.org/garden

NATIONAL AGRICULTURAL LIBRARY (US): nal.usda.gov/legacy/afsic/community-gardening

Wild Habitat Creation

BUILDING A 'SANDARIUM': ptes.org/my-garden/how-to-make-a-habitat-for-ground-nesting-bees/

BUILDING A SIMPLE, SAFE BEE HOUSE: foxleas.com/wild-bees-and-gardens.asp

CREATING A BOG GARDEN: discoverwildlife.com/how-to/wildlife-gardening/how-to-make-a-bog-garden-for-wildlife/

CREATING A MINI POND: wildlifetrusts.org/actions/how-create-mini-pond

DEAD HEDGING: en.wikipedia.org/wiki/dead_hedge

HEDGES: rhs.org.uk/plants/articles/misc/best-native-shrubs-for-hedging

LOG PILES: rspb.org.uk/get-involved/activities/nature-on-your-doorstep/garden-activities/create-a-log-pile-for-wildlife/

MAKING COB BRICKS: youtube.com/watch?v=dAksl8Z6JaM&t=17s

Planting Suggestions

ROSYBEE SIX YEAR STUDY:
rosybee.com/research-study

ROYAL BOTANIC GARDEN KEW:
kew.org/read-and-watch/how-to-attract-pollinators

ROYAL HORTICULTURAL SOCIETY: rhs.org.uk/science/conservation-biodiversity/wildlife/plants-for-pollinators

THE XERCES SOCIETY (USA): xerces.org/pollinator-conservation/pollinator-friendly-plant-lists

organiccatalogue.com
primrose.co.uk
groworganic.com (US)
planetnatural.com (US)

SPECIALIST BEE HABITATS: BOXES, NESTS AND SUPPLIES
birdfood.co.uk/solitary-bee nest-box
masonbees.co.uk
nurturing-nature.co.uk (widely cited as the best on the market)
crownbees.com (US)
osmiabee.com (US)

Recommended Suppliers

PLANTS, PLUGS AND SEEDS
beehappyplants.co.uk
britishwildflowermeadowseeds.co.uk
heritageseeds.co.uk
jekkasherbfarm.com
meadowmania.co.uk
realseeds.co.uk
rocketgardens.co.uk
rosybee.com
seedsofitaly.com (organic range)
wildflowerturf.co.uk
anniesheirloomseeds.com (US)
johnnyseeds.com (US)

OTHER GARDENING PRODUCTS
gardening-naturally.com
gardentower.co.uk
naturalgrower.co.uk

CHAPTER 9

—

INDEX OF PLANTS
Mentioned in this Book

Achillea (*Achillea* spp.)

A. *millefolium* 'Proa'

A. *ptarmica* 'The Pearl'

Balkan Yarrow (*A. clypeolata*)

Common Yarrow (*A. millefolium*)

Egyptian Yarrow (*A. taygetea*)

Fern Leaf Yarrow (*A. filipendulina* 'Cloth of Gold')

Woolly Yarrow (*A. tomentosa*)

Aconitum (*Aconitum* spp.)

A. *carmichaelii*

A. *napellus*

A. *n. henryi* 'Sparks variety'

Agastache (*Agastache* spp.)

A. 'Black Adder'

A. 'Blue Boa'

Anise Hyssop (*A. foeniculum*)

Korean Mint (*A. rugosa*)

Alder (*Alnus* spp.)

Common Black Alder (*A. glutinosa*)

Italian Alder (*A. cordata*)

Alexander (*Smyrnium olusatrum*)

Alfalfa (*Medicago sativa*)

Alkanet (*Alkanna tinctoria*)

Allium (*Allium*)

Alsike Clover (*Trifolium hybrida*)

American Holly (*Ilex opaca*)

Anemone (*Anemone* spp.)

Garden Anemone (*A. coronaria*)

Winter Windflower (*A. blanda*)

Wood Anemone (*A. nemorosa*)

Angelica (*Angelica archangelica*)

Anise Hyssop (*Agastache foeniculum*)

Apple (*Malus* spp.)

Crab Apple (*M. sylvestris*)

M. *domestica*

M. *pumila*

Aquilegia (*Aquilegia* spp.)

Artemisia (*Artemisia vulgaris*)

Artichoke (*Cynara cardunculus* var. *scolymus*)

Ash (*Fraxinus* spp.)

Asters

Blue Wood Aster (*Symphyotrichum*)

Calico Aster (*Aster lateriflorus*)

Chamomiles (inc. *Anthemis tinctoria*)

Michaelmas Daisy (*Aster* × *frikartii* 'Mönch')

New York Aster (*A. novi-belgii*)

Sea Aster (*A. tripolium*)

White Wood Aster (*Eurybia divaricate*)

Aubretia (*Aubrieta deltoidea*)

Autumn Hawkbit (*Scorzoneroides autumnalis*)

Azalea (*Rhododendron* spp.)

Balkan Yarrow (*Achillea clypeolata*)

Baptisia (*Baptisia* spp.)

Barberry (*Berberis* spp.)

Basil (*Osimum* spp.)

Greek Basil (*O. var. minimum*)

Holy Basil/Tulsi (*O. tenuiflorum*)

Thai Basil (*O. basilicum* var. *thyrsiflora*)

Bay (*Laurus nobilis*)

Beach Rose (*Rosa rugosa*)

Bean family (*Phaseolus* spp.)

Bee Balm (*Monarda* spp.)

Scarlet Bee Balm (*M. didyma*)

Spotted Bee Balm (*M. punctata*)

Wild Bergamot (*M. fistulosa*)

Bee Orchid (*Ophrys apifera*)

Beech (*Fagus* spp.)

Begonia (*Begonia* spp.)

Bell Heather (*Erica cinerea*)

Bellflower (*Campanula* spp.)

Canterbury Bells (*C. medium*)

Carpathian Bellflower (*C. carpatica*)

Clustered Bellflower (*C. glomerata*)

Harebells (*C. rotundifolia*)

Nettle-leaved Bellflower (*C. trachelium*)

Peach-leaved Bellflower (*C. persicifolia*)

Rampions (*C. rapunculus*)

Berberis (*Berberis vulgaris*)

Bergamot (*Monarda* spp.)

Scarlet Bee Balm (*M. didyma*)

Spotted Bee Balm (*M. punctata*)

Wild Bergamot (*M. fistulosa*)

Betony (*Stachys officinalis*)

Bilberry (*Vaccinium myrtillus*)

Birch (*Betula* spp.)

Bird Cherry (*Prunus avium*)

Bird's-foot Trefoil (*Lotus corniculatus*)

Bistort (*Persicaria* spp.)

Common Bistort (*P. bistorta*)

Redshank (*P. maculosa*)

Black-eyed Susan (*Rudbeckia hirta*)

Black-eyed Susan Vine (*Thunbergia alata*)

Black Horehound (*Ballota nigra*)

Black Locust (*Robinia Pseudoacacia*)

Blackberry (*Rubus fruticosus*)

Blackcurrant (*Ribes nigrum*)

Blackthorn (*Prunus spinosa*)

Blanketflower (*Gaillardia* spp.)

Blazing Star (*Liatris spicata*)

Blessed Milk Thistle (*Silybum marianum*)

Blue Wood Aster (*Symphyotrichum*)

Bluebells (*Hyacinthoides no-scripta*)

Blueberry (*Vaccinium* spp.)

European Blueberry/Bilberry (*V. myrtillus*)

Boneset (*Eupatorium perfoliatum*)

Borage (*Borago officinalis*)

Boston Ivy (*Parthenocissus tricuspidata*)

Box (*Buxus*)

Bracken (*Pteridium*)

Bramble (*Rubus fruticosus*)

Bristly Ox Tongue (*Helminthotheca echioides*)

Broad Bean/Fava Bean (*Vicia faba*)

Broom (*Cytisus* spp.)

Portuguese Broom (*C. multiflorus*)

Wild and Cultivated Broom (*C. scoparius*)

Buddleja (*Buddleja* spp.)

Orange Ball Tree (*B. globosa*)

Weyer Butterfly Bush (*B. × weyeriana*)

wild and cultivated (*B. davidii*)

Bugle (*Ajuga reptans*)

Burdock (*Arctium* spp.)

Burnet/Scottish Rose (*Rosa spinossima*)

Busy Lizzie (*Impatiens walleriana*)

Buttercups (*Ranunculus acris*)

Calamint, Lesser (*Calamintha nepeta*)

Calendula (*Calendula* spp.)

Pot Marigold (*C. officinalis*)

Calico Aster (*Aster lateriflorus*)

Californian lilac (*Ceanothus*)

Campanula (*Campanula*)

Campion, Red (*Silene dioica*)

Canadian/Red Maple (*Acer rubrum*)

Canterbury Bells (*Campanula medium*)

Cardoon (*Cynara cardunculus*)

Carpathian Bellflower (*Campanula carpatica*)

Carrot family (Apiaceae)

Catmint (*Nepeta* spp.)

Garden Catmint (*N. × fassenii*)

Lesser Calamint (*Calamintha nepeta*)

Cat's Ear (*Hypochaeris radicata*)

Ceanothus/Californian lilac (*Ceanothus* spp.)

Chamomiles

Corn Chamomile (*Anthemis arvensis*)

German Chamomile (*Matricaria chamomilla*)

Golden Marguerite *Anthemis tinctoria*)

Roman Chamomile (*Chamaemelum nobile*)

Charlock (*Sinapis arvensis*)

Cherry (*Prunus* spp.)

    Bird/Wild Cherry (*P. avium*)

    Blackthorn (*P. spinosa*)

    Sour Cherry (*P. cerasus*)

    Wild Cherry (*P. padus*)

    Yoshino Cherry (*P. × yedoensis*)

Chestnuts

    Horse Chestnut (*Aesculus hippocastanum*)

    Sweet Chestnut (*Castanea sativa*)

Chickpeas (*Cicer arietinum*)

Chicory (*Cichorium intybus*)

Chilli Pepper (*Capsicum frutescens*)

Chives (*Allium schoenoprasum*)

Christmas Rose (*Helleborus niger*)

Clary Sage (*Salvia sclarea*)

Clematis (*Clematis* spp.)

    Golden Clematis (*C. tangutica*)

    Winter Jasmine (*C. cirrhosa*)

Clovers (*Trifolium* spp.)

    Alsike Clover (*T. hybrida*)

    Red Clover (*T. pratense*)

    Sweet Yellow Clover (*Melilotus officinalis*)

    White or Dutch Clover (*T. pratense*)

Clustered bellflower (*Campanula glomerata*)

Comfrey (*Symphytum officinale*)

Coneflower *see* Echinacea

Coreopsis (*Coreopsis* spp.)

Coriander/Cilantro (*Coriandrum sativum*)

Corn Chamomile (*Anthemis arvensis*)

Cornflower (*Centaurea* spp.)

    Annual Wild Cornflower (*C. cyanus*)

    Greater Knapweed (*C. scabiosa*)

    Knapweed (*C. nigra*)

    Perennial Mountain Cornflower (*C. montana*)

    Sweet Sultan (*C. moschata*)

Cotoneaster (*Cotoneaster* spp.)

    Cotoneaster Tree (*C. frigidus*)

    Creeping Cotoneaster (*C. adpressus*)

    Hedge Cotoneaster (*C. lucidus*)

    Wall Cotoneaster (*C. horizontalis*)

Courgette/Zucchini (*Cucurbita pepo*)

Cow Parsley (*Anthriscus sylvestris*)

Crab Apple (*Malus sylvestris*)

Cranesbill (*Geranium* spp.)

    Meadow Cranesbill (*G. pratense*)

    Spotted Cranesbill (*G. maculatum*)

    Striped Bloody Cranesbill

    (*G. sanguineum* var. *striatum*)

Creeping Rosemary (*Salvia rosmarinus*,

    formerly *Rosmarinus officinalis*)

    Prostratus Group

Creeping Thistle (*Cirsium arvense*)

Crocus (*Crocus* spp.)

    C. vernus

    Autumn Crocus (*C. sativus*)

Currants (*Ribes* spp.)

    Blackcurrant (*R. nigrum*)

    Flowering currant (*R. sanguinem*)

    Redcurrant/Whitecurrant (*R. rubrum*)

Daffodils (*Narcissus* spp.)

Dahlia (*Dahlia* spp.)

Daisies (Asteraceae)

    Lawn/Common Daisy (*Bellis perennis*)

    Michaelmas Daisy (*Aster amellus*)

Dandelion, Common (*Taraxacum officinale*)

Deadnettle (*Lamium* spp.)

    Red Deadnettle (*L. purpureum*)

    Spotted Deadnettle (*L. maculatum*)

    White Deadnettle (*L. album*)

Delphinium (*Delphinium*)

    Larkspur (*Consolida ajacis*)

Devil's Bit Scabious (*Succisa pratensis*)

Dill (*Anethum graveolens*)

Dog Rose (*Rosa canina*)

Dogwood (*Cornus sanguinea*)

Dutch Clover (*Trifolium pratense*)

Echinacea (*Echinacea* spp.)

Echium (*Echium* spp.)

    Giant/Tree Echium (*E. pininana*)

    Viper's Bugloss (*E. vulgare*)

    Viper's Bugloss 'Blue Bedder'

    (*E. vulgare* 'Blue Bedder')

Egyptian Yarrow (*Achillea taygetea*)

Elderberry (*Sambucus*)

Eupatorium (*Eupatorium* spp.)

    Boneset (*E. perfoliatum*)

    Hemp Agrimony (*E. cannabinum*)

Euphorbia (*Euphorbia*)

Eyebright (*Euphrasia* spp.)

Fava Beans/Broad Beans (*Vicia faba*)

Fennel (*Foeniculum* spp.)

    Common Fennel (*F. vulgare*)

    Sweet Fennel (*F. v.* var. *dulce*)

Field Maple (*Acer campestre*)

Field Scabious (*Knautia arvensis*)

Figworts (*Scrophularia* spp.)

    S. nodosa

Fleabane, Common (*Pilicaria dysenterica*)

Foxglove (*Digitalis* spp.)

    Native Foxglove (*D. purpurea*)

    Small-flowered Foxglove (*D. parviflora*)

    Woolly Foxglove (*D. lanata*)

French Marigold (*Tagetes patula*)

Fuchsia (*Fuchsia* spp.)

Gaillardia (*Gaillardia* spp.)

Gallberry/Inberry (*Ilex glabra*)

Garlic Mustard (*Alliaria petiolate*)

Geranium, Hardy (*Geranium* spp.)

    G. 'Rozanne'

Herb Robert (*G. robertianum*)

Meadow Cranesbill (*G. pratense*)

Meadow Cranesbill 'Striatum' and 'Spinners'

    (*G. pratense* 'Striatum' and 'Spinners')

Spotted Cranesbill (*G. maculatum*)

Spotted Cranesbill 'Beth Chatto'

    (*G. maculatum* 'Beth Chatto')

Striped Bloody Cranesbill (*G. sanguineum*

    var. *striatum*)

German Chamomile (*Matricaria chamomilla*)

Germander (*Teucrium*)

Globe Thistle (*Echinops* spp.)

    Glandular Globe Thistle (*E. sphaerocephalus*)

    Hungarian Globe Thistle (*E. bannaticus*)

Goat/Pussy Willow (*Salix caprea*)

Goldenrod (*Solidago* spp.)

    Canada Goldenrod (*Solidago canadensis*)

Gooseberry (*Ribes uva-crispa*)

Gorse (*Ulex europaeus*)

Grape Hyacinth (*Muscari* spp.)

    Common Grape Hyacinth (*M. neglectum*)

Great Mullein (*Verbascum Thapsus*)

Greek Basil (*Osimum* var. *minimum*)

Grey Willow (*Salix cinerea*)

Ground Elder (*Aegopodium podagraria*)

Ground Ivy (*Glechoma hederacea*)

Hairy Willow Weed (*Epilobium hirsutum*)

Hardy Geraniums/Cranesbills (*Geranium* spp.)

    G. 'Rozanne'

    Herb Robert (*G. robertianum*)

    Meadow Cranesbill (*G. pratense*)

    Meadow Cranesbill 'Striatum' and 'Spinners'

        (*G. pratense* 'Striatum' and 'Spinners')

    Spotted Cranesbill (*G. maculatum*)

    Spotted Cranesbill 'Beth Chatto'

        (*G. maculatum* 'Beth Chatto')

Striped Bloody Cranesbill (*G. sanguineum* var. *striatum*)

Harebells (*Campanula rotundifolia*)

Hawkbit (*Leontodon* spp.)

Autumn Hawkbit (*Scorzoneroides autumnalis*)

Hawksbeard (*Crepis* spp.)

Beaked Hawksbeard (*C. vesicaria*)

Rough Hawksbeard (*C. biennis*)

Smooth Hawksbeard (*C. capillaris*)

Hawthorn (*Crataegus* spp.)

Common Hawthorn (*C. monogyna*)

Midland Hawthorn (*C. laevigata*)

Hazel *(Corylus)*

Heath Dog Violet (*Viola canina*)

Heathers

Autumn/Winter Heather (*Erica carnea*)

Bell Heather (*E. cinerea*)

Cross Leaf Heather (*E. tetralix*)

Ling (*Calluna vulgaris*)

Hebe (*Hebe* spp.)

H. 'Autumn Glory'

New Zealand Lilac (*H. hulkeana*)

Short Tubed Hebe (*H. brachysiphon*)

Hedge Woundwort (*Stachys sylvatica*)

Helenium (*Helenium* spp.)

Hellebores (*Helleborus* spp.)

Christmas Rose (*H. niger*)

Green Hellebore (*H. viridis*)

Helleborus × ballardiae

H. × hybridus

H. × sahinii 'Winterbells'

Lenten Rose (*H. orientalis*)

Stinking Hellebore (*H. foetidus*)

Hemp Agrimony (*Eupatorium cannabinum*)

Herb Robert (*Geranium robertianum*)

Hibiscus (*Hibiscus* spp.)

Hoary Plantain (*Plantago media*)

Hogweed (*Heracleum sphondylium*)

Holly (*Ilex* spp.)

American Holly (*I. opaca*)

Common Holly (*I. aquifolium*)

Inberry/Gallberry (*I. glabra*)

Japanese Boxleaf Holly (*I. crenata*)

Holy Basil/Tulsi (*Osimum tenuiflorum*)

Honeysuckle (*Lonicera* spp.)

Common Honeysuckle (*L. periclymenum*)

Japanese Honeysuckle (*L. japonica*)

Trumpet Honeysuckle (*L. sempervirens*)

Winter Honeysuckle (*L. fragrantissima*)

Horehound, Black (*Ballota nigra*)

Horse Chestnut (*Aesculus hippocastanum*)

Horseshoe Vetch (*Hippocrepis comosa*)

Hydrangea, Climbing (*Hydrangea anomala petiolaris*)

Hyssop (*Hyssopus officinalis*)

Ice Plant (*Sedum spectabile*)

Inberry/Gallberry (*Ilex glabra*)

Iris (*Iris* spp.)

Blue Flag Iris (*I. versicolor*)

Blue Skullcap (*Scutellaria lateriflora*)

Yellow Flag Iris (*I. pseudacorus*)

Italian Alder (*Alnus cordata*)

Ivy, Flowering (*Hedera* spp.)

English Ivy (*H. helix*)

Persian Ivy (*H. colchica*)

Japanese Allspice (*Chimonanthus praecox*)

Japanese Boxleaf Holly (*Ilex crenata*)

Japanese Lime (*Tilia maximowicziana*)

Japanese Quince (*Chaenomeles japonica*)

Japonica (*Camellia japonica*)

Jasmine (*Jasminum* spp.)

Common Jasmine (*J. officinale*)

Winter Jasmine (*J. nudiflorum*)

Kale (*Brassica oleracea* Acephala Group)

Kidney Vetch (*Anthyllis vulneraria*)

Knapweed (*Centaurea* spp.)

Common Knapweed (*C. nigra*)

Greater Knapweed (*C. scabiosa*)

Macedonian Knapweed (*Knautia Macedonia*)

Korean Mint (*Agastache rugosa*)

Laburnum (*Laburnum* spp.)

Lamb's Ear (*Stachys byzantina*)

Larkspur (*Delphinium*)

Lavender (*Lavandula* spp.)

Edelweiss Lavender (*L.* 'Edelweiss')

English Lavender (*L. angustifolia*)

Lavandula × *intermedia* 'Hidcote Giant'

Leeks (*Allium porrum*)

Round-headed Leek (*A. sphaerocephalon*)

Lemon Balm (*Melissa officinalis*)

Lenten Rose (*Helleborus orientalis*)

Liatris (*Liatris spicata*)

Lilac (*Syringa* spp.)

Lime (*Tilia* spp.)

European Lime (*T.* × *europeaea*)

Japanese Lime (*T. maximowicziana*)

Large-leaved Lime (*T. platyphyllos*)

Small-leaved Lime (*T. cordata*)

Linden (*Tilia*)

Ling (*Calluna vulgaris*)

Lingonberry (*Vaccinium vitis-idaea*)

Loosestrife

Purple Loosestrife (*Lythrum salicaria*)

Yellow Loosestrife (*Lysimachia vulgaris*)

Lungwort (*Pulmonaria*)

Common Lungwort (*P. officinalis*)

Pulmonaria 'Opal' (*P. officinalis* 'Opal')

White Corolla Red Lungwort (*P. rubra* var.*albocorollata*)

Macedonian Knapweed (*Knautia Macedonia*)

Mahonia (*Mahonia* spp.)

Mahonia × *media*

Oregon Grape (*M. aquifolium*)

Mallow, Common (*Malva sylvestris*)

Maple (*Acer* spp.)

Canadian/Red Maple (*A. rubrum*)

Field Maple (*A. campestre*)

Marjoram (*Origanum* spp.)

Sweet Marjoram (*O. majorana*)

Wild Marjoram (*O. vulgare*)

Marsh Mallow (*Althaea officinalis*)

Marsh Marigold (*Caltha palustris*)

Marsh Thistle (*Cirsium dissectum*)

Marsh Woundwort (*Stachys palustris*)

Meadow Cranesbill (*Geranium pratense*)

Meadow Rue, Purple (*Thalictrum dasycarpum*)

Meadow Vetchling (*Lathyrus pratensis*)

Melilot (*Melilotus* spp.)

Michaelmas Daisy (*Aster* × *frikartii* 'Mönch')

Midland hawthorn (*Crataegus Laevigata*)

Mignonette (*Reseda*)

Mint (Lamiaceae family)

Mint (*Mentha* spp.)

Mountain Mints (*Pycnanthemum* spp.)

Peppermint (*M.* × *piperita*)

Spearmint (*M. spicata*)

Monk's Hood (*Aconitum* spp.)

Carmichael's monk's hood (*A. carmichaelii*)

A. napellus

Aconitum 'Spark's Variety' (*A. napellus henryi* 'Sparks Variety')

Mountain Mints (*Pycnanthemum* spp.)

Mustard, Wild (*Sinapsis arvensis*)

Nasturtium (*Tropaeolum majus*)

Nepeta

Garden Catmint (*Nepeta* × *fassenii*)

Lesser Calamint (*Calamintha nepeta*)

Nettle-leaved Bellflower (*Campanula trachelium*)

Nettles

Common Nettle (*Urtica dioica*)

Red Hemp Nettle (*Galeopsis angustifolia*)

New York Aster (*Aster novi-belgii*)

New Zealand Lilac (*Hebe hulkeana*)

Oak (*Quercus*)

Oilseed Rape (*Brassica napus oleifera*)

Onion family (*Allium* spp.)

Chives (*A. schoenoprasum*)

Leek (*A. porrum*)

Onion (*A. cepa*)

Sicilian Honey Garlic (*A. siculum*)

Opium Poppy (*Papaver somniferum*)

Orchid, Bee (*Ophrys apifera*)

Oregano (*Origanum* spp.)

Sweet Marjoram (*O. majorana*)

Syrian Oregano (*O. syriacum*)

Wild Marjoram (*O. vulgare*)

Oregon Grape (*Mahonia aquifolium*)

Parsnips (*Pastinaca sativa*)

Passiflora (*Passiflora* spp.)

Common Passionflower (*P. caerulea*)

Passion Fruit (*P. edulis*)

True Passionflower (*P. incarnata*)

Pea family (Fabaceae)

Peach (*Prunus persica*)

Peach-leaved Bellflower (*Campanula persicifolia*)

Pear (*Pyrus* spp.)

Peas (*Pisum sativum*)

Pelargonium (*Pelargonium* spp.)

Peppermint (*Mentha* × *piperita*)

Periwinkle (*Vinca*)

Phacelia (*Phacelia tanacetifolia*)

Plantain, Hoary (*Plantago media*)

Plum (*Prunus* spp.)

Plume Thistle (*Cirsium rivulare* 'Atropurpureum')

Poppy (*Papavar* spp.)

Common/Field Poppy (*P. rhoeas*)

Opium Poppy (*P. somniferum*)

Portuguese Broom (*Cytisus multiflorus*)

Pot Marigold (*Calendula officinalis*)

Primrose (*Primula vulgaris*)

Primula (*Primula*)

Common Primula (*P. vulgaris*)

Cowslip (*P. veris*)

Oxlip (*P. elatior*)

Privet (*Ligustrum* spp.)

Garden Privet (*L. ovalifolium*)

Wild Privet (*L. vulgare*)

Purple Loosestrife (*Lythrum salicaria*)

Purple Meadow Rue (*Thalictrum dasycarpum*)

Purple Toadflax (*Linaria purpurea*)

Pussy Willow (*Salix* spp.)

Pyracantha (*Pyracantha*)

Queen Anne's Lace (*Daucus carota*)

Radish (*Raphanus* spp.)

Ragworts (*Senecio* spp.)

Rampions (*Campanula rapunculus*)

Rapeseed (*Brassica napus*)

Raspberry (*Rubus idaeus*)

Red Campion (*Silene dioica*)

Red Clover (*Trifolium pratense*)

Red Hemp Nettle (*Galeopsis angustifolia*)

Red Maple/Canadian (*Acer rubrum*)

Redcurrant (*Ribes rubrum*)

Redshank (*Persicaria maculosa*)

Restharrow (*Ononis repens*)

Rhododendron (*Rhododendron* spp.)

Robinia (False Acacia), Black Locust
(*Robinia Pseudoacacia*)

Rocket, Wild (*Diplotaxis tenuifolia*)

Roman Chamomile (*Chamaemelum nobile*)

Rose Campion (*Lychnis coronaria*)

Rosebay Willow Herb (*Chamerion
angustifolium*)

Rosemary (*Salvia rosmarinus,*
formerly *Rosmarinus officinalis*)

Roses (*Rosa* spp.)

Beach Rose (*R. rugosa*)

Burnet/Scottish Rose (*R. spinossima*)

Dog Rose (*R. canina*)

Harsh Downy-rose (*R. tomentosa*)

Prickly Wild Rose (*R. Acicularis*)

Sweet Briar/Eglantine (*R. rugibinosa*)

Roses, Climbing (*Rosa* spp.)

R. 'Bobbie James'

R. filipes 'Kiftsgate'

R. moschata

R. polyantha 'Grandiflora'

R. 'Rambling Rector'

Roses, Rambling (*Rosa* spp.), *Rosa*
'Kew Rambler'

Rudbeckia (*Rudbeckia* spp.)

Black-eyed Susan (*R. hirta*)

R. fulgida var. *sullivantii* 'Goldsturm'

Runner Beans (*Phaseolus coccineus*)

Russian Sage (*Perovskia atriplicifolia*)

Russian Vine (*Fallopia baldschuanica*)

S age (*Salvia* spp.)

Common Sage (*S. officinalis*)

Russian Sage (*S. yangii*, previously known as
Perovskia)

Sainfoin (*Onobrychis viciifolia*)

St John's Wort (*Hypericum mutilum*)

Sallow (*Salix* spp.)

Salvia (*Salvia* spp.)

Balkan Clary (*S. nemorosa* 'Ostfriesland')

Clary Sage (*S. sclarea*)

Crested Sage (*S. viridis*)

Rosemary (*S. rosmarinus,* formerly
Rosmarinus officinalis)

Russian Sage (*S. yangii,* formerly
Perovskia atriplicifolia)

Salvia 'Amistad'

Salvia × *sylvestris* 'Caradonna'

Woodland Sage (*Salvia nemorosa*)

Scabious (*Scabious/Knautia* spp.)

Field Scabious (*K. arvensis*)

Greater Knapweed (*Centaurea scabiosa*)

Macedonian Knapweed (*K. Macedonia*)

Scorpion Senna (*Hippocrepis emerus*)

Scottish Bluebells (*Campanula rotundifolia*)

Scottish Rose/Burnet (*Rosa spinossima*)

Sea Aster (*Aster tripolium*)

Sea Holly (*Eryngium* spp.)

Alpine Sea Holly (*E. alpinum*)

Big Blue Sea Holly (*E. zabelii* 'Big Blue')

Flat Sea Holly (*E. planum*)

Miss Willmott's Ghost (*E. giganteum*)

Tripartite Sea Holly (*E.* × *tripartitum*)

Wild Sea Holly (*E. maritimum*)

Sea Kale (*Crambe maritima/Crambe cordifolia*)

Sea Lavender (*Limonium vulgare*)

Sedum (*Sedum* spp.)

Ice Plant (*S. spectabile*)

Ice Plant 'Autumn Joy' (*S. spectabile*
'Autumn Joy')

Orpine (*S. telephium* 'Matrona')

Two-row Stonecrop (*S. spurium*)

White Stonecrop (*S. album*)

Selfheal (*Prunella vulgaris*)

Sheep's Bit Scabious (*Jasione montana*)

Sicilian Honey Garlic (*Allium siculum*)

Silver Birch (*Betula pendula*)

Skullcap (*Scutellaria* spp.)

  Blue Skullcap (*S. lateriflora*)

  Common Skullcap (*S. galericulata*)

Sneezeweed (*Helenium* spp.)

Snowberry (*Symphoricarpos albus*)

Snowdrops (*Galanthus* spp.)

  Common Snowdrop (*G. nivalis*)

Sour Cherry (*Prunus cerasus*)

Sow Thistle (*Sonchus* spp.)

Soybeans (*Glycine max*)

Spear Thistle (*Cirsium vulgare*)

Spearmint (*Mentha spicata*)

Speedwell (*Veronica*)

  Garden Speedwell (*V. longifolia*)

  Spiked Speedwell (*V. spicata*)

  Wild Speedwell (*V. chamaedrys*)

Spotted Cranesbill (*Geranium maculatum*)

Spurge (*Euphorbia*)

Squash family, including Courgette, Marrow, Pumpkin, etc (*Cucurbitae* spp.)

Stachys (*Stachys* spp.)

  Betony (*S. officinalis*)

  Betony 'Hummelo' (*S. officinalis* 'Hummelo')

  Hedge Woundwort (*S. sylvatica*)

  Lamb's Ear (*S. byzantina*)

Stinking Hellebore (*Helleborus foetidus*)

Stonecrop (*Sedum*)

Strawberry (*Fragaria* spp.)

Striped Bloody Cranesbill (*Geranium sanguineum* var. *striatum*)

Sunflower (*Helianthus annuus*)

Sweet Chestnut (*Castanea sativa*)

Sweet Clover (*Melilotus* spp.)

Sweet Pea (*Lathyrus odoratus*)

Sweet Sultan (*Centaurea moschata*)

Sweet Yellow Clover (*Melilotus officinalis*)

Sycamore (*Acer pseudoplatanus*)

Syrian Oregano (*Oregano syriacum*)

Tansy (*Tanacetum vulgare*)

Teasels (*Dipsacus* spp.)

Thai Basil (*Osimum basilicum* var. *thyrsiflora*)

Thistle family

  Alpine Sea Holly (*Eryngium alpinum*)

  Big Blue Sea Holly (*E. zabelii* 'Big Blue')

  Blessed Milk Thistle (*Silybum marianum*)

  Creeping Thistle (*Cirsium arvense*)

  Echinops ritro 'Veitch's Blue'

  Eryngium × *tripartitum*

  E. zabelii 'Big Blue'

  Flat Sea Holly (*E. planum*)

  Glandular Globe Thistle (*Echinops sphaerocephalus*)

  Hungarian Globe Thistle (*E. bannaticus*)

  Marsh Thistle (*Cirsium dissectum*)

  Miss Willmott's Ghost (*Eryngium giganteum*)

  Plume Thistle (*Cirsium rivulare* 'Atropurpureum')

  Spear Thistle (*C. vulgare*)

  Tripartite Sea Holly (*Eryngium* × *tripartitum*)

  Wild Sea Holly (*E. maritimum*)

Thrift (*Armeria* spp.)

Thyme (*Thymus* spp.)

  Conehead Thyme (*T. capitatus*)

  Garden Thyme (*T. vulgaris*)

  Lemon Thyme (*T.* × *citriodorus*)

  Wild Thyme (*T. polytrichus*)

Tickseed (*Coreopsis* spp.)

Toadflax, Purple (*Linaria purpurea*)

Tomatoes (*Solanum lycopersicum*)

Tree Lupin (*Lupinus arboreus*)

Trefoils

  Bird's-foot Trefoil (*Lotus corniculatus*)

  Lesser Trefoil (*Trifolium dubium*)

Turnip, White (*Brassica rapa rapa*)

Umbellifers, wild (parsley/carrot family)

Alexanders (*Smyrnium olusatrum*)

Angelica (*Angelica archangelica*)

Cow Parsley (*Anthriscus sylvestris*)

Hogweed (*Heracleum sphondylium*)

Queen Anne's Lace (*Daucus carota*)

Wild Parsnip (*Pastinaca sativa*)

Verbena (*Verbena* spp.)

Argentinian Vervain (*V. bonariensis*)

Slender Vervain (*V. rigida*)

Trailing Verbena (*V. speciosa* 'Imagination')

Verbena 'Peaches and Cream' (*V. hybrida*
'Peaches and Cream')

Veronica (*Veronica* spp.)

Garden Speedwell (*V. longifolia*)

Spiked Speedwell (*V. spicata*)

Wild Speedwell (*V. chamaedrys*)

Vervain (*Verbena*)

Argentinian Vervain (*V. bonariensis*)

Slender Vervain (*V. rigida*)

Vetches (*Vicia* spp.)

Common Vetch (*V. sativa*)

Horseshoe Vetch (*Hippocrepis comosa*)

Kidney Vetch (*Anthyllis vulneraria*)

Meadow Vetchling (*Lathyrus pratensis*)

Viburnum (*Viburnum*)

Violets (*Viola* spp.)

Common Dog Violet (*V. riviana purpurea*)

Heath Dog Violet (*V. canina*)

Horned Violet (*V. cornuta*)

Sweet Violet (*V. odorata*)

Viper's Bugloss (*Echium vulgare*)

Wallflower (*Erysimum* spp.)

Common Wallflower (*E. Cheiranthus*)

Perennial Wallflower (*E. bicolor*
'Bowles Mauve')

Water Avens (*Geum rivale*)

Water Figwort (*Scrophularia auriculata*)

Water Mint (*Mentha aquatica*)

Watercress (*Nasturtium officinale*)

Wayfaring tree (*Viburnum lantana*)

Weeping Willow (*Salix babylonica*)

Weigela (*Weigela* spp.)

Weyer Butterfly Bush (*Buddleja × weyeriana*)

White Wood Aster (*Eurybia divaricate*)

Whitecurrant (*Ribes rubrum*)

Wild Mustard (*Sinapis arvensis*)

Wild Rocket (*Diplotaxis tenuifolia*)

Wild Strawberry Tree (*Arbutus unedo*)

Willow (*Salix* spp.)

Goat/Pussy Willow (*S. caprea*)

Grey Willow (*S. cinerea*)

Weeping Willow (*S. babylonica*)

Willow Herb

Hairy Willow Weed (*Epilobium hirsutum*)

Rosebay Willow Herb (*Chamerion
angustifolium*)

Winter Aconite (*Eranthis hyemalis*)

Winter Honeysuckle (*Lonicera fragrantissima*)

Winter Windflower (*Anemone blanda*)

Wintersweet (*Chimonanthus praecox*)

Wisteria (*Wisteria*)

Wood Anemone (*Anemone nemorosa*)

Wood Sage (*Teucrium scorodonia*)

Woodland Sage (*Salvia Nemorosa*)

Woolly Yarrow (*Achillea tomentosa*)

Yarrow (*Achillea* spp.)

Balkan Yarrow (*A. clypeolata*)

Common Yarrow (*A. millefolium*)

Egyptian Yarrow (*A. taygetea*)

Fern Leaf Yarrow (*A. filipendulina*
'Cloth of Gold')

Woolly Yarrow (*A. tomentosa*)

ACKNOWLEDGEMENTS

Bee Information Sources

My bookshelves are buckling under the weight of books about wild bees, some of the best of which I have listed on pages 188–193. My research also drew on many websites of painstaking field work and observation, and I regularly disappeared down rabbit holes following citations and links to scientific papers.

But many bee species, particularly the solitaries, are still not that well understood, and expert opinions can differ on fundamentals. My rule of thumb was therefore to find at least two additional corroborating sources before incorporating any information.

I asked knowledgeable people to help me unpick some puzzles. Of special mention for their rapid responses are my husband Dale Gibson, Stephen Fleming, editor of *BeeCraft* magazine, and Professor Mark Winston on whose (virtual) doorstep I arrived one evening with an urgent question about cocoons and 'bee silk'. Incredibly kindly, he emailed me straight back with a definitive answer. Professor Dave Goulson and I also had a long, fascinating discussion about organic land management, bumblebee farming and the increasingly abrasive relationship between beekeepers and wild bee conservationists. My special thanks to all of the above for their time and thought-provoking input.

A Year of Upheaval

On a more personal note, thanks as ever to the brilliant editorial team at Quadrille Books for their unwavering encouragement, which kept me going as I researched and wrote this book through a particularly trying year in which Dale and I sold our London home and business premises, found a country location, moved 18 years' worth of accumulated everything and quickly got ourselves up and running again. It's been real!

A thank you too to Lynda and Geoff Kinsella, from whom we inherited the tremendous Essex garden in which we are now finding our feet.

And finally, again, my love and thanks to Dale. Husband of too many decades to mention, provider of plenty from the kitchen garden, indulger of my wilder projects, possessor of a fine critical eye and – always – my strongest, and wittiest, supporter.

Managing Director Sarah Lavelle
Senior Commissioning Editor Harriet Butt
Designer Maeve Bargman
Photographer Maria Bell
Illustrator Claire Hurrup
Head of Production Stephen Lang
Senior Production Controller Sabeena Atchia

Published in 2023 by Quadrille,
an imprint of Hardie Grant Publishing

Quadrille
52–54 Southwark Street
London SE1 1UN
quadrille.com

Text © Sarah Wyndham Lewis 2023
Photography © Maria Bell 2023
Design © Quadrille 2023

ISBN 978 178 713 918 3

Printed using soy inks in China